Africans in Canada: Blending Canadian and African Lifestyles?

Peter Ateh-Afac Fossungu

Langaa Research & Publishing CIG
Mankon, Bamenda

Publisher
Langaa RPCIG
Langaa Research & Publishing Common Initiative Group
P.O. Box 902 Mankon
Bamenda
North West Region
Cameroon
Langaagrp@gmail.com
www.langaa-rpcig.net

Distributed in and outside N. America by African Books Collective
orders@africanbookscollective.com
www.africanbookcollective.com

ISBN: 9956-790-44-3

DISCLAIMER

All views expressed in this publication are those of the author and do not necessarily reflect the views of Langaa RPCIG.

Table of Contents

iv

Introduction

Book's Driving Forces

I write this book solely because of my concern for the future of children and social work departments that have enormous powers over the making or ruining of the future of children (whatever the definition attached). I talk of Africa and Canada specifically but I think the message applies around the globe. I write from the perspective of a child that has been through it and seen it all and would not want other children to have to go through what I have had to go through. No child should have to go through all what I went through simply because of some particular individual's selective definition of family or child; a designation, moreover, that would be exclusively geared toward making readily available resources for educating children unavailable to some children. A child must not be considered a child by the parents only insofar as the child's services are concerned but regarded not as a child when it comes to the education and other needs of that child. I was able to surmount some of these ill-conceived definitions and other road-blocking devices largely because of some inborn powers. Not every child has those. And, even in regard of the survival strategies I learnt or quickly developed, that capacity to learn and adapt too can never be the same with all children, as is amply evidenced in the numerous cases in the book. I also write from the viewpoint of a parent who is concerned about the way some parents are using children as mere means of acquiring revenue from or tools of punishing the other parent; and they persist in doing so to the total disregard of the future of said children who paradoxically do not even feature in their un-African and un-Canadian definition of family. Social work departments are also enjoined to ensure that, in addition to having the academic qualifications, people working for them do satisfy some basic minimum attributes incidental to what their job is all about.

Family is defined variously by some experts as (1) a basic social unit consisting of parents and their children, considered as a group, whether dwelling together or not: *the traditional family;* or a social unit consisting of one or more adults together with the children they care for: *a single-parent family;* (2) the children of one person or one couple collectively: *We want a large family;* (3) the spouse and children of one person: *We're taking the family on vacation next week;* (4) any group of persons closely related by blood, as parents, children, uncles, aunts, and cousins: *to marry into a socially prominent family;* and (5) all those persons considered as descendants of a common progenitor.[1] In human context, a **family** (from Latin: *familia*) is a group of people affiliated by consanguinity, affinity, or co-residence. In most societies it is the principal institution for the socialization of children. Anthropologists most generally classify family organization as matrilocal (a mother and her children); conjugal (a husband, his wife, and children; also called nuclear family); and consanguineal (also called an extended family) in which parents and children co-reside with other members of one parent's family.[2] Two types of family units dominate in this book, namely, the nuclear that is predominant in Canada and other Western societies and the extended that is most prominent in Africa.

This book's story cuts across continents (Africa and North America) though being heavily set in Cameroon, yet, with far-flung consequences for and in Canada. Its whole essence is pitched on how children's life and future are seriously affected by the way family (and marriage) would be defined especially by parents and other relations. The book's "principles" are of general application although its story is personal and true, revolving around the author and his "family". The story is worth the telling because of its potentials, inter alia, for motivating and helping many people who might learn from the author's intriguing experiences. It is not so much about the story, captivating (with some parts of it perhaps unbelievable to Canadians)

---

[1] See http://dictionary.reference.com/browse/family.
[2] http://en.wikipedia.org/wiki/Family.

as it is; but so much about the rare strategies that have aided author in surmounting obstacles (some being really life-threatening) and moving on in life. Most of these stumbling blocks are clearly and simply the result of the inconsiderate way some parents, partners, and other relations define family and children (and marriage).

Background and Importance of Story and Its Lessons

As a child growing up, I always wanted to become, first, a pilot; second, a medical doctor; and, third, a judge/lawyer. Why I ended up with the third rather than the others could begin to explain this book's whole essence – the definition of family and the way such characterization affects the future of children. As a young child, aeroplanes have always fascinated me and I wanted to fly one myself one day. That is why I took my lessons in the sciences (especially mathematics and physics) in secondary school very seriously, becoming one of the few students selected on merits to do additional maths in Saint Joseph's College, Sasse, Buea (hereinafter Sasse College). Furthermore, I always dream (even until date) and find myself actually flying without wings; and most often flying to escape from some sort of danger below. The pilot profession literally had nothing to do with what I considered even then as my objective in life – bringing more happiness to the greatest number of persons possible – that greatly influenced the other two choices. I would not be talking much about those choices in this book as I would about defining myself with my objective; a goal that was born out of my innate gratitude and recognition that I was the one chosen out of so many disadvantageously placed village children whose chances of ever seeing a school classroom were very close to naught – not because they were intellectually incapable but solely because of the handicap called financial means. Because of this money issue, the advance toward my objective almost came to a stop in Cameroon College of Arts and Sciences (CCAS) Kumba: but for the fact that I knew myself well and what I was up to and up against in the household.

According to sociologists and linguists, the social unit that lives in a house is known as a *household*. Most commonly, a household is a family unit of some kind, though households may be other social groups, organizations, or individuals. This book uses household throughout to signify a family unit such as ours.yes, the availability of financial means has always been an obstacle to my speedy realisation of goals in and out of the household; not really because those means were not there but solely because of the selective and inconsistent meaning parents attached to 'family' and 'child'. And I hardly fell within that meaning, notwithstanding that I have never myself felt like I was not a child of the household, by deeds or thoughts. My "outsider" status coupled so well with my likeability to spell a lot of unnecessary money issues for me. But, as it is popularly said in Cameroon's *lingua franca* (what some denigrate as Pidgin but I prefer to call Njangawatok[3]), *cow weh noh get tail na God di drivam fly*. This could almost be likened to what Fossungu (1998a: 5) describes when he states that "It is common for people born with infirmity... to make up for it by [highly] developing in another less suitable area." A lot of people seem to believe or think that money is the singular ingredient of success in life. Many often talk about money in terms that would make you think happiness in life completely depends on the quantity of it that you have or spend. While not denying the importance of money, this book questions its primacy to success in certain fields such as becoming educated; showing that there are far more important personal attributes to success and happiness than just having the money on-hand. You will discover that if everything had to depend on money, I would never have acquired high school education, let alone set foot in a university amphitheatre. Of course, money has been one of the major obstacles to my smooth progress to acquiring university education but it has not been the only; nor

---

[3] For more on this (Njangawatok) language that is being audaciously proposed for elevation to a 'national-unity' language in Cameroon, see Fossungu (2013a: 161-166). You will surely encounter its use a lot in this book.

have the multiple negative forces completely succeeded in barring me from the attainment of some of my objectives. Why?

Most people who know me just do not know me at all; and this includes the woman I eventually ended up with as wife. Most of them do not have an idea of what I have been through to be where I am. That is why many people around me just cannot figure out how I am able to carry on, bitter-free, after all what they know as having recently happened in my life, including insults and disillusioning comportment from those I dearly love. That is one of the many reasons I tell this story so as to share some of my ingredients of and strategies for surviving adversity. Some are inborn, others are learnt and acquired. This is certainly not the first book written with such a goal in mind (see, e.g., For-Mukwai, 2010); but I think the most important thing to the matter is to know exactly who you are. Knowing so, and having objectives with which you define yourself, would make things a lot easier since your worth is also known to you.

Some of my friends have not been able to hide their amazement, sometimes even wondering aloud: "How come he is having so *many* academic degrees and certificates and yet would not only do odd jobs but also does so with much pride?" When this particular question often comes to my attention, I think the following to myself: If this query was posed to one of the elders in the village of Nwangong (Cameroon), the sure short response in Njangawatok would be *Na condition e make njanga e back e bend* (It is tough times that bent the shrimp's back). But then that does not quite explicate things since that short elderly reply can also mean that the shrimp had been doing nothing and, consequently, tough times caused its back to bend; which is a very different thing from saying that the shrimp itself bent its back in order to counter or weather those menacing conditions just like Chinua Achebe's little bird, *nza*, justifying that it has learnt to fly without perching because men have learnt to shoot without missing. This book finds a home more in the second than in the first category.

The book's lessons are many but I think the main lesson (from which many others radiate in all directions) that you should take home, whatever your academic discipline or professional career, is that when you are destined for great accomplishments, there is nothing that can stop you except you. If this book teaches parents generally but divorcing or divorced ones specifically that the future and interest of the children, whatever the cause of their going apart (or calculations for the non-divorcing others), should always be the prime mover for whatever arrangement (or decision) they do or should make, then it would have achieved one of its purposes. In short, I think the world would be a better place if people generally look at the larger picture of things; because larger picture people are usually not only pioneers of bigger projects but also are better suited to give children, without definitional distinctions, a better or brighter future than what they themselves have, irrespective of their societies.

With all the focus on the definitions of family (and marriage) as they impinge on the future of children and social work, Chapter 1 examines some strategies for surviving and progressing within the intricacies of the African family in which defining a child took more than a single connotation from both parents for different purposes. It acquaints you with the foundational bases of my successes and failures from the angle of my unique family setting and upbringing, as well as from the direction of some important early family relations. It furnishes a good background that greatly aids in a better comprehension of the arguments in the rest of the book that would expose the 'un-African' and 'un-Canadian' definition of family and the consequences on the future of children and social work in both Canada and Africa in chapters 2-5.Chapter 2 studies the short-cutting of the African family money and other complications to obtain university education; a short-cut that chapter 3 shows was elongated by the bombshell of African family hurdles, a blow that initiated the roaming days that also occasioned the ideal-spouse flop, leading up to eventual spouse's wholly new 'un-African' and 'un-Canadian' definition of family. Chapter 4 examines the make-or-break year in Manjo, a year exacerbated by the spouse fiasco and university age-limit. Chapter 5 tackles the family issues, examining boldness, truthfulness and the spouse quest from the angle of the marriage decision (the parties' or the families'?), using some interesting responses from a Bangwa royal family. There is, of course, the conclusion.

Chapter 1

Progressing Within African Family Intricacies: Confronting the Truth about Yourself and Understanding the Problem Confronting You

Knowing that it is not my story *per se* that is important here, but the lessons learnt and drawn from it, I will like to go with the story behind the lessons rather than the lessons behind the story. You cannot know yourself until you can confront the truth about yourself and also about those you deal with. If you are not afraid of your own truth, you will hardly be scared of someone else's truth. Those who tell the truth about themselves do not do so to get pity and/or praise; only those who tell lies do. You do not hurt by telling the truth; it is the truth (that you have learnt to embrace) that hurts. If you learn to embrace the truth, you will seldom be hurt by it. This book, for example, could still have been written as a fictional story but I think that would be a big lie since I would be telling you my story without actually letting you know it is my story. There are certainly many other facts of my life that cannot all be brought in and must be left out, not with the intention of hiding them. There is no part of my complex life that I am ashamed of. On the contrary, I take a lot of pride in my multi-dimensional life, an invaluable source of strength for me. If much has not been brought in here, it is simply because of "the well-known fact from Davidson that the writing of history [moreover one as multifaceted as mine] would in any case become a hopeless venture if it involved explaining everything" (Fossungu, 2013a: 5).I cannot even begin to tell you just how hard it has been to sift through it all to come out with just what you now have in front of you.

When you know what you are up against, you will often correctly anticipate problems before they actually come. There is thus nothing as easy as solving a problem that pops up when you are ready for it.

1

What makes a problem really bad and daunting is when it takes you by surprise. You are caught off guard. Once you know who you are, it becomes very easy to know who or what you are dealing with. For instance, if I already know myself, there is no need to get angry or become bitter if someone describes me exactly as I am. Concretely, if I have a big clock-ticking head, and you tell me that I have that, there is no need for me to be angry about that. But if I did not know that, then I might be really angry. If I know exactly the type of head I have, and you tell me: "You are really making good use of that your big clock-ticking head," then I will be happy that I am not wasting God's gift to me.

On the other hand, if you describe me as what I know I am not, there will still be no need for me to get annoyed because your description can never change me from what I know to be me to your description. Thus, describing my head that I very well know as "small, empty and oblong" does not need to make me angry because your saying so can never change the shape and content of my head as I know it to be. With an outlook like this on life, you will hardly have problems facing the truth and with others because you will know as well that telling them that they are what they are not, will never make them what they are not. Furthermore, a good knowledge of yourself and situation reduces your reliance on a lot of professionals. I am by no means saying that you should never go and see a therapist, for example. All I am saying is that your therapy (if not the cure itself) begins with you understanding yourself and situation. This is great wisdom that I have gained over the years; and would next be sharing with you through my large extended royal family generally but particularly my two sets of parents.

Two Sets of Parents

Most people traditionally have just one father and one mother; I have more than that; not to mention the complex web of brothers and sisters, uncles and aunts, nieces and nephews, cousins, and friends. I was born in 1960 in Nwangong to a couple but brought up

2

(from the age of about six) by another couple in the coast or what is known as *ncheng* in Bangwa. The Bangwa are in South West Region of Cameroon and Fossungu (2013b: 119) thinks that their federalist tradition would also mainly explain their numerous palaces, wondering why Cameroon's administrators appear to have been infected only by the love of these palaces but not by the federalism that is behind the palaces. Nwangong, often referred to as Fossungu (the name of its fon or paramount chief), is one of nine fondoms that constitute the Bangwa ethnic group. These chiefdoms or fondoms are known today under these names (which are actually mostly titles of their paramount chiefs or fons – to distinguish from the many other sub-chiefs): Fonjumetaw, Fontem, Foreke Cha Cha, Fossungu, Fotabong, Fotabong II, Foto, Fozimombin, and Fozimondi (Fossungu, 2013b: 121-122).[1] Nwangong is ruled by the Fon or Paramount Chief. Limiting to those that I know, Fon Sunday Tendongmo Fossungu was succeeded in 1979 by Fon David Foncha Fossungu who was also succeeded in 2008 by Fon Nicasius Nguazong Fossungu. Traditionally, the last two are also still my grandfathers but I would not be using grandpa for them, also distinguishing all of them by abbreviating their respective first two names (such as Fon ST Fossungu, Fon DF Fossungu, and Fon NN Fossungu).

I have a lot of parents, grandparents, sisters, brothers, aunts and uncles (some of them you will meet later) who never went too far in, or at all to, school. But I cannot help marvelling when some of them open their mouths to talk. Take for instance Fon ST Fossungu who many in the family and out of it have described in terms that would fit those of King Solomon in the bible. As young as I then was, I still remember a lot of things he used to do or say while I was growing up in and around the palace. But take for now an example out of the palace when he was visiting my father for the first time, since my departure from Nwangong and arrival in Victoria (Cameroon). He said that people who *always* conform to what others say or think have

---

[1] For more on these Bangwa fondoms, see Brain (1972).

no idea of who they really are. As a young lad listening to him from a distance talking to other elders, I tried to make sense of what he had said but was not sure I got it. So when the crowd had thinned out a little bit, I approached and requested to ask the Fon something.

Everyone in his entourage was sort of furious at "this child without manners and fear of elders" and beckoning me off. But the Fon, to their astonishment, hushed them down and asked me what I wanted to know. Not wanting the others to hear, I approached and whispered in his ear my question as to what he meant by what I have outlined above. He was himself so surprised that, at my age (I was then about ten or eleven), I had been listening to, and following, their conversation. My grandfather stared at me hard and then laughingly said: "Because every individual must have something that sets them apart from the rest of us;" observing that he had always known I was going to be like my father. "Which of my two fathers," I asked aloud. At this point a deafening silence fell into the living room and I then realized not only grandpa (but also some uncles in his entourage that I knew very well but had pretended not to know) heard the question. I quickly ran out to continue with the dishes I had been washing, knowing well that what I had just said must be hurting some of them in the same way as this book may affect some others, including my parents and siblings.

The De Facto Family

It seems to me that anyone who has had the privilege of living the type of life I have and had the kind of relationships I have would naturally not define father, mother, brother, sister, and child (family, in short) in the very restricted way most people and academic disciplines do. Some would consider it a negative but I often find things positive in things that a lot of people will consider negative, such as effectively having two fathers and two mothers; four parents, that is. My *ncheng* upbringing was precisely in three different towns in the South West Region of Cameroon: Victoria, Muyuka, and Kumba; the two parents of this upbringing being known in this book as my

4

mother and father (or papa) – the other two obviously carrying birth
or biological before them.

Thecla Anangafac Fosungu (Née Njumo)

In the royal family a few people have adopted the 'Fosungu'
version of the family name but the majority would go with the
'Fossungu' option. Known in this book as my mother or Mami
Thecla, she studied in one of the most prestigious girls-only Catholic
Mission secondary schools – Queen of Rosary Secondary School,
Okoyong in Mamfe (South West Region). Going as far as form four,
she dropped out due to pregnancy. Mami Thecla occupies a very
important place in my life; and I put her in this position not just
because she is the mother who brought me up. Of especial
importance is the fact that she provoked my very first "defining
moment" as a very special kid destined for great accomplishments.

Mami Thecla was known in the palace and village as Mami *Ncheng*
(Mom from the coast), respected and held in high esteem, if not for
her own sake, then because of her *massa* or husband. The number of
fowls, pigs, and goats that went about crying and begging for their
lives to be spared when she often arrived in the palace was equalled
to none. It was always feasting in the palace from when she landed till
when she took off. Her *massa* rarely came as he was working and she
therefore did almost all of the coming and going. But even her
massa's arrival did not bring as much joy to the children as hers
because, as it is often said, mothers often know better what children
like and want – justifying in a way well known African musician
Prince Nico Mbarga's *Sweet Mother*. Apart from the candies and
cookies and other such goodies, I brightly remember how Mami
Thecla would usually not eat much of the sumptuous and assorted
food from the numerous wives of the Fon and those of the Fon's
children; but she also often made sure the rest of the food was out of
the reach of the hawk-like adults; only us children being served it.
How could she be anything but dear to us children?

5

Imagine then how special and blessed you will feel when one of Mami Thecla's trips to Nwangong is solely for the purpose of taking just you (among all the so many children) to *ncheng* where you will thereafter be living, not just a temporary visit. This is the 1960s I am talking about, not the village of today where cars even come to every hour and minute; and it is not like Mami Thecla arrives today and makes the announcement and the next day you are on the way. She spends a whole week or so before departure in the course of which you are the centre of attention, of admiration, of adoration, of advice given left and right, and of special association with Mami Thecla. Truly a defining moment, it was.

Whenever she came, she stayed at the house of Cecilia Asongu Fossungu (Mami Cecilia) whose only son, Uncle David Ntimah Fossungu (henceforth Uncle Ntimah), was then living with her in *ncheng*. This time was not different and I remember spending three straight days at Mami Cecilia's at Mami Thecla's demand. Any village child would have paid a lot to be there in that manner but not this clock-ticking-headed boy; for I kept wondering what the reason for the three-day house change was, despite the boost it gave to my being special in the eyes of the others. Did Mami Thecla want to find out for herself just how obedient or foolish or intelligent I was? Whatever it was she was finding out, I am sure my inborn powers worked well for me and I passed the test as she had let me return home with indication that we were leaving in two days.

Mami Thecla is special to me, in addition, because she is the one to whom my birth mother personally handed me over. Gravitating her importance to higher grounds is also the fact that she is the prime mover behind most of the events that have altered (for good or for bad) the course of the lives of so many people; all hinged on her definition of family and children. And the affected people also include not only the children of the household and those that spent time in it, but as well the entire Fossungu royal family, many members of which would see Mami Thecla as unloving, egoistic, scheming, and uncaring. I, for one, cannot say Mami Thecla did not like or love me. There are two especial reasons.

First, she would not have been the one who (still breastfeeding her little baby boy called Bernard Mbancho Fosungu) came to get me from the village. I think Mami Thecla could be summed up as the one woman that has greatly impacted on my life by not understanding and appreciating me for who I really am (e.g., as a child who never saw her in any other terms than a mother); this misunderstanding having had across-the-board consequences on most of my junior brothers and sisters of the household whom I raised and babysat. Coming behind Joseph Njumo Fosungu is Bernard (that you have just met) who is followed, in order, by Beatrice Nguikem Fosungu; Annastasia Chamo Fosungu; Maureen Nkengafac Fosungu; Gladys Mazano Fosungu; Quinta Alonche Fosungu; and Justine Mamefat Fosungu who was born almost at the same time with Delphine Fosungu from my father's other younger wife, Julie Fosungu. Marie-Claire Efuelancha Fossungu, a cousin, adds to the list, having lived with us from when she entered secondary school in the early 80s to graduation at the university in the early 90s. The few older children in the household at the time I arrived there were: Therese Nkengafac Fosungu; Josephine Forzi Fosungu; Vincent Akana Fonwancheng, the son of my father's friend (and the man from whom I got all my names, except the family one); Uncle Ntimah (Mami Cecilia's son you have already met); and Michael Njumo, my mother's younger brother. The last two were not there for long after my arrival, most probably because they had soon completed primary school and left the household.

Mami Thecla, moreover, could not have hated me because I am a very likeable person and do not know anyone that has had the chance to be with me even for a short time and did not like me. My likeability, I know, is simply infectious and has often put me into lots of trouble, including the definitional one unfolding here. I think my mother's main problem (stemming from the likeability?) was her fear that I was a threat to her *own* birth children. It seems to be a protective motherly trait, as you will see in many other moms (including my own birth mother) in due course. I cannot exactly explain why most mothers behave that way but I can explain why I

7

say Mami Thecla's fear seemed to have dominated all her dealings with or concerning me. Because of her failure to manage this fear (founded or unfounded) she was unable to see that I was rather a shinning guide, than an obstacle, to her birth children's progress and future; children that she also appears to have intoxicated in my regard. I therefore became the greatest 'sinner' when my father (her *massa*) sang my praises particularly as I not only did just the right things papa wanted but also (since I did not share in their fear of him or anyone else) quickly understood him more than my brothers and sisters who would be quick to describe him as difficult; which is quite true if you do not understand Emmanuel Nguajong Fosungu.

Emmanuel Nguajong Fosungu (Chief Forbehndia)

Papa was born in 1931 and died on 11 October 2002. Studying in the then British Southern Cameroons and in Nigeria to become a statistician, he returned home to West Cameroon and began working with the West Cameroon electricity corporation, Powercam (which later became Sonel: *Société nationale de l'élétricité*), until his retirement in the late 80s.

I have had so many defining moments in my life. But my most memorable defining moment (that also concretely cemented my main objective in life) is this conversation I had with my father in Kumba – and which also makes the important point about papa's financial means – regarding his always letting his tenants (and he had a lot of them in Yoke, Kumba, and Victoria) who had not paid their rents for so long to go scot-free. Don't you think, papa, I thought aloud to him, that doing so would encourage other tenants not to also pay and at the end go free? Papa had a particular look and smile that always lid his face whenever I asked him one of those my hooky questions and this time was no exception. He then said son (or better P) those who have no intention of paying their rents would still not pay – whether or not they know I let one tenant off the hook. In this life people are not the same (I was wondering here if it was not my grandpa speaking). By the way, papa pursued, you see Mr. Lucas has

8

not paid all his rents for the last six or so months. The good thing though is that all his children are still in school and doing very well too, like you, my son. If their father has any small amount of brains, my father went on, he will be thankful and I myself, I am happy that he is not giving me my rents which I clearly deserve to have but he is not using it unproductively. Therefore, P, he concluded, I am not only sending you and your other siblings to school; I am also doing so in a way to the children of Mr. Lucas.

Wow! I could not help but see an angel talking to me right then in the image of my dad. I said simply: "Thank you papa for opening my eyes; in fact, I would like to be like you when I grow up." He replied: "You don't need to grow up to be like me; and you don't need to be like me but to be better than me. That is the only way you could ever thank me," he concluded, quickly leaving the scene before I could ask any more questions. I was transfixed for a while reflecting on all what had just transpired. Some of the things that immediately struck me were the way papa looked at the larger picture of things, not the narrow; not judging B from A's action; and not restricting the net of help to just his own family and relations. All of these and more have greatly impacted on my outlook. If I could describe papa in just one sentence, I would simply say he was a far-sighted and scrupulous man, with a second religion called farming, who indeed liked helping people without limitation as to family ties – attributes that obviously did not sit well with his somewhat narrow-minded partner and her own extended family.

Three things need to be clarified here for a better grasp of this African extended family concept. The first is that all the uncles and aunts in this book bearing Fossungu are in reality my father's half-siblings since the Fon had so many wives, with some of them like my father's mother bearing only one child for him; second, that we usually referred to those of them that came to live with us in the household as "Brother" or "Sister" X although I will be using the appropriate "Uncle" or "Aunty" X in this book; and, third, that some of them like Uncle Vincent Temenu Fossungu later became Chief Fonenge and switched from the regular royal family name to their

9

own. Because his first name seems to be the most favourite name within my family circles, I would prefer using only the nobility name of those of them who have one, such as Foletia (meaning Chief of Letia quarter in Nwangong) who, otherwise, is Uncle Vincent Aghendia Fossungu. That brings us full circle to papa's narrow-minded partner and in-laws.

Indeed, Aunty Constance Tumekong Fossungu (henceforth Aunty Tumekong), who lived with us for a while in the household in Yoke, is even known to have mused that it was as if since papa could not say no to anyone that arrived his home, conditions in the house had been fashioned to make they themselves say no to staying. This aunty seems to have observed well and she captures as well the astonishment of many in the royal family and village as to how I have been able to academically achieve as much as I have, living and growing up in the household. As you will see throughout this book, the two young boys *of* the household especially were socialized to promoting the "Us-Them"[2] dichotomy that conveniently created the 'invisible hand' decision of many of the 'them' to 'quit the household by themselves'. Many of the 'them' that would have gained from this unique man's desire to help people have thus been barred by papa's partner who does not seem to share his perspectives and would instead have made the household very intolerable to those that her definition of family clearly labels "outsiders" and parasitic "children with dead fathers".

This is quickly seen right away in the case of Marie-Claire. Another "outsider", Marie-Claire almost left the household in Victoria like many others before and after her: but for my timely intervention and *her willingness* to listen and learn. I found Marie-Claire one day weeping and on the verge of packing her small bag and leaving. I asked her why she was in that state of mind and she sobbed even more, explaining how the boys *of* the household (Joseph and

---

[2]Katerina K. Frantzi, "Human Rights Education: The United Nations Endeavour and the Importance of Childhood and Intelligent Sympathy" 5:1 *International Education Journal* (2004),cited in Fossungu (2013a: 52).

Bernard) had insultingly labelled us as "children whose fathers have all died and they are here eating our father's money." She was astonished when I demanded if that was just what was making her cry that much and about to go away, almost pitting me on the other side, not hers.

"My dear little sister," I said to her, "stop your crying and let's go to the nearby store and get some candies." Away from the house and making sure that no one was eavesdropping, I asked again what we were called that made Marie-Claire cry and she repeated it. "Is it not true that your father and mine are dead and that *their* father is bringing us up?" Marie-Claire began weeping again and I sternly told her to go and pack and leave if she does not want to learn anything at all. I think sometimes you need those you consider your friends to fling the truth into your face for you to see truth, and not insult. That is what real friends are for. I had therefore emphasized to Marie-Claire: "By the way, before you go, know that I would be without any tears today if I had to weep over everything like you are now doing. Remember also that I will always be here 'eating' that money, no matter what, until papa himself tells me to leave; and if you think your late father was very foolish in personally bringing you here when he did, I don't think papa was stupid in sending for me after my own [biological] father died." I then told her to go and pack if that was what she wanted to do with her life but she had already made up her mind to stay, knowing that success was hers "as long as I have you as my brilliant and courageous guide." I told her she had a deal and that I was proud of her. And I am truly proud of Marie-Claire for being the first to listen and learn. Because she could listen and learn (unlike many similarly counselled before and after her), today she is the only other "outsider" that has made it to university graduation in the household despite all the stream of insults about dead fathers like Karlemon Tale'eh Fossungu, one of my birth parents.

The Biological Connexion

Karlemon Mbugnyi Tale'eh Fossungu

He is my dead birth father. As I have said, and as you will see further, the most foundational ingredient of my success in and out of the household has been the fact of confronting the truth about me head on without qualms, and making the best out of it. I have already talked briefly about the father who cared for and nurtured me and now is the time to say something about my birth or biological father who I do not quite know – in the sense of not having his image in my mind. My lack of physiological knowledge of him is not because I was too young to know him when, after his death, I left Nwangong for the city of Victoria (now contentiously called Limbe[3]). He was almost never there at home since, being the first son of Fon ST Fossungu and therefore the heir apparent to the throne, he was always journeying to represent his father or do some errands for him.

Although I am currently the first of his children, I understand that I was actually about the eighth or tenth (from biological mother's side). The story even goes that I might have been (or be) this troublesome baby (an *obanje* in one of Chinua Achebe's novels), going and coming and going just to upset the parents; explaining some marks that were put on me at birth so that I would be recognized if I returned (again). Could it really be that I am an *obanje* that refused to go only because of the marks on one of my ears and neck? How come I *have four eyes* (that is, easily see what others don't see), a characteristic traditionally attributed to *obanjes?* My birth mother however answers with a different story. In her own words, while "I was 'shitting' the children, *they* were picking them up and eating like a hawk does to a hen's chickens." Who 'they' is referring to, I have never gotten anyone who has been willing to explain, notwithstanding all efforts; not even from my birth mother over

---

[3] For further studies on this contention that is grounded in the calculated assimilation of the English-speaking minority in Cameroon, see Fossungu (2013a: 166-168).

whom my biological father is said to have fought such a ferocious battle.

Regina Akiefac Fossungu (née Fonge)

Known in this book as Mami Regina or my birth mother, she was born in 1931; giving birth to me at the age of twenty-nine. Although I have not grown up with her, she is the first influence in my life; with her influences having greatly aided my shaping of the other later influences in unimaginable ways. Furthermore, she and I do not often feel like we never grew up together physically, notwithstanding that being the case. Although papa was not used to letting me know, I was aware of the "messages" (helping financially) she often sent to him through visiting uncles, who also always passed on my own small private "messages" from her. Mami Regina regularly came down to Yoke to help with farm work and on such occasions I got to know certain things about her from our casual conversations; still remembering a lot also from the time I spent with her before my departure for the household in Victoria.

Very hardworking and full of unimaginable strength, Mami Regina is highly intelligent. I remember her once telling me in Yoke that she always knew I was going to stick to the pieces of advice she had given to me. Mami Regina and I understand each other so well even without talking that I often wonder if we communicate by telepathy. I have never told her anything concerning the tribulations in the household. She has never behaved as if she was concerned that there could be trouble. But I remember her asking me one day in Yoke how I was doing (*Allekoh*, in Bangwa). I simply said "I am very grateful for the pieces of advice you gave me in the village; they have been very helpful." She too merely said "I know." I did not ask how she knew. Most mums who do not understand their son the way she does would have wanted to know how helpful, as well as the son wishing to know how the knowledge came about.

Mami Regina has this uniquely strange way of seeming to know what I am thinking and usually stops the questioning before I start asking. It seems to me she is intelligently protecting me from

13

something by hiding something from and about me. Often, as soon as I say 'Mami', she cuts in with "Ateh-Afac will one day kill me with his questions." I usually then keep off my query because she and I both know somehow that something is not okay but at the same time we both also understand (*sans aucune discussion*) the need not to know, at least for the time being. It seems that my father and several others in the royal family are astutely part of this conspiracy to keep me ignorant of whatever it is. I know very well that Mami Regina trusts me a lot and knows that I am not a trouble maker; but sometimes I get this feeling when I look at her that she is very concerned about losing me to what or over what, I cannot tell. This often happens when I look her straight into the eyes and she asks with much concern: "What, Ateh-Afac?" I love looking at her like that for no other reason than to enjoy her innate beauty and charm that even old age and hard times have not been able to dry out.

My biological mum is said to have loved being the centre of attention and her prettiness and other rare qualities duly gave her that position. Popularly known as Mama Regie, she would fit what Americans would separately call a singing, dancing, and beauty, queen. I still fondly remember her singing while she would be bulldozing on the farm around Letia to which she usually took us, her two little boys. In her youthful days she was a real hot cake, with the competition for her being so fierce – my birth father, of course, being in that ferocious struggle. Fonenge has been of some little aid here. As he once explained to me in a brief interview on the Fossungu family, in order to outwit the other competitors, my birth father had "carried" Mami Regina; meaning that he had 'forcefully eloped' with her before coming after alone to formally ask for her hand in marriage from the parents. Women naturally find it easier talking about some of these things to their daughters-in-law than to their own sons, as was the case with my wife, Scholastica Achankeng Asahchop, mother of two of my children – Ngunyi Ateh-Afac Fossungu and Nguajong Forbehndia Fossungu. Scholastica once told me that Mami Regina had explained to her that my birth father was not really her first choice but that "the way he had acted certainly

14

won my heart and earned him the place." Who were or could be the other competitors for Mami Regina that my birth father outwitted?

This question is important to ask because most of my uncles have evaded responding to it; and also because the circumstances surrounding my birth father's death have never been clear or explained to me as no one has bothered to let me know. Uncle Richard Ngufor Fossungu (henceforth Uncle Ngufor) who even talked about it, on being asked, merely stated to me that he fell from a palm tree and sustained some injuries that later killed him. But I cannot remember seeing my birth father lying sick at home at any time. I can still remember the day my birth father died. I had a premonition that something really wrong had happened. Although we (children) were then not allowed to come close to where there was a corpse, things were happening so fast that day. For example, the way we were rounded up and taken to a compound out of the palace; the general commotion and near confusion provoked by the extraordinary Night Society (or *Etough*[4]); all told me that it was not normal. Of course, said abnormality could all have been due to the fact of his being the first son of the Fon. Nevertheless, the suspicious manner through which my birth father must have died dawns on me whenever I look back at some facts, four of which would suffice here.

First, hardly had Tale'eh Fossungu been gone when some of his brothers (my uncles) started coming home every night and "beating up" his wife. 'Beating up' is the way that a young innocent child would describe 'having sex with' because of the mother's crying or groaning he often hears at night whenever any of those uncles comes around. I remember once supposedly going to my birth mother's rescue only to be sent off with the uncle's painful slap and angry rebuke for even daring to come there. I would imagine that Dieudonné Asongu Fossungu must have seen a whole lot of the

---

[4]According Brain (1972: 6), the Night Society in Bangwa is the feared arm of the law, the secret weapon of the fon who carries out fearful punishment on witches, adulterers, and murderers.

15

'beating ups' of mother and other such traumatizing acts that, until his death in June 2011, he could hardly hold on to any of the two wives that successively came into his life. Dieudonné is the only sibling with whom I share both biological parents but he is not the only blood sibling I have.

Esther Asongkeng Fossungu and Vincent Awandem Fossungu also have the same biological father with me; their own mother having been his second wife. I never had the chance to know my mother's *mbanya* (appellation for the other woman/women that have the same *massa* with you). Quite apart from my not being a nose-poker, I did not know my birth father had a second wife and the wife also most probably because both co-spouses were not living together or in the same household. Of course, I knew "Awandem" well in the palace as one other favourite grandchild to the King Solomon of Nwangong (the others including "Ateh-Afac" – me). But I only knew that the second wife's two children were my half-siblings in 1994. This was after my sister's tearful trip to Douala where I was then based. Imagine meeting a blood sister you never knew you had at Uncle Ngufor's in Douala, casually greeting her like anyone else and taking off; only to learn later how much she had cried before returning to Ekona (in South West Region); the sole purpose of her trip to Douala (in Littoral Region) having been to see her senior brother just back from Canada whom she thought knew exactly who she was to him. Why didn't anybody present her to me, I had asked Uncle Ngufor whose response was that they thought I knew her. I was truly overwhelmed and only God knows how I was able to drive to Ekona that day, as unplanned as the journey was. I will leave the rest of what happened in Ekona (where my sister is the second wife of a man with a large family) to your imagination.

Second, I remember too well my very first return to the village in the early 80s, after high school. Uncle William Asongu Fossungu (is my younger brother, Dieudonné, named after him?) – who had long chased mother and brother away and *owned* my birth father's compound in the village and who was the first to start the 'beating up' – spent all the time trying to discover if I knew this or that. All

16

through his sneaky interviews I feigned ignorance and saw how contented he was that I did not know anything about the village when I had left it. Ignorance is at times a very powerful tool and a virtue.

Third, in the late 80s (I was then teaching in the Yaoundé University), while in the village one day as a grown up man and without prefacing it with 'Mami', I confronted my birth mother with the question: What happened to my dad? We were just two of us in the house that evening; but she became so frightened, looking around as if there were more people in the room than just the two of us, shaking and saying the following almost to herself: "Please, God, help me; with this kind of questioning *they* would also take his head!" I do not know who this *they* stands for but, seeing how shaken she was, knowing I was right there in the village, and recalling all the village witchcraft stories that had led papa not to be taking his children (including me) to the village for so long, I desisted from pursuing the topic further.

Fourth, my suspicion on Tale'eh's apprehensive death would seem to be confirmed also through the children he left behind and I am sure my ignorance of their blood relations to me for so long could be some sort of helpful ignorance or an ingredient of my progress. In October 2002 I gathered the other three siblings and we headed to Nwangong for a cleansing ritual because it was said that we, and especially Awandem, were wandering a lot due to the fact that our birth father had not been replaced or succeeded. That was the general belief and talk going around and Esther particularly pleaded with me that this should be done as I was then around, with it not being possible without me. So we were in the village for that purpose and my initial idea had been to let Awandem be the successor since I am not based in Cameroon. But thank God that I have this hunch that I often follow almost religiously and which (as you will further see) has proven to be an indispensable component of success to me in a lot of domains. At the last minute when Fon DF Fossungu wanted to know who was to be the new Tale'eh, I indicated it was me. God alone knows why this happened because my

17

three blood siblings (but Awandem particularly) had, unknown to me, teamed up with other elders involved with the ceremony, insisting that our father's succession could not have any sense until the preliminary question of his place of abode had first been settled.

I had never till then seen a lion except in books and on television (though I would not say that in the village as the belief there is that saying no to anyone that asks if you have seen a certain animal invites his or her showing you one, being him or herself transformed). But I saw one in Uncle William sitting right there. Up to this day I do not know if others saw what I saw but I am sure I am right in what I saw – an excessively angry lion ready to devour whoever stood in his way. Uncle William's anger must have been on two fronts, should my siblings' insistence or suggestion be followed: (1) public knowledge of what had happened that he is now on my birth father's land and property and (2) my not buying adjacent land from him to increase the one I already had in Letia quarter as per a previous plan with him. I am very sure none of Tale'eh's four children would have left the village alive if I had also joined the chorus or let Awandem be the successor of our biological father.

I had therefore told everyone present that I did not come all the way from Canada to fight over any land or property left behind by whosoever; that I was capable of acquiring same for my siblings and myself. Therefore, I had concluded, let Uncle William get the witnesses for the Letia land sale so that we could quickly close that up and go on with the main ceremony that had brought us all there that day. You could actually feel the dangerous tension that had already built up in the air then rapidly loosening up and falling apart and the lion reassuming its human form, happy at the turn of events. When Awandem and the others (perhaps because they know much more than I do – virtuous ignorance) continued privately to complain to me that our father's property could not just have been surrendered in that way, I dryly inquired: "What is this property that you guys value more than your lives?"

From that day Nkemtale'eh became my nobility name; deriving from when I formally succeeded my birth father, becoming Tale'eh,

18

in the ceremony during which Fon DF Fossungu (perhaps in appreciating the manner I had wisely and far-sightedly handled every catastrophe that was just waiting to unfold) also surprisingly bestowed on me the title of *nkem* or notable of the village and adviser to the Fon. I say surprisingly because people usually lobby a lot to have some of these titles but I had done none of those things and was completely unaware of the Fon's intention prior to the surprise. In Nwangong therefore you will hardly hear anyone addressing me in any other name other than Dr. Nkemtale'eh; this being that same little village boy whose future Mami Thecla greatly helped to chart and define, wittingly or otherwise, within the framework of a household with a second religion called farming.

Surviving With Papa's Religion Across Continents: Backing Academics With Farming

Papa was clearly not a farmer of circumstances but indeed a farmer at heart. Farming was simply a religion in the household, and my ability to practise it well has been an invaluable ingredient of success, most often almost overshadowing my non-inclusion within the meaning of 'child' or 'family'. Farming did not just back up my academic progress but actually charted the chequered course of my education, both positively and negatively. I was able to subdue the negative forces most probably because (unlike many others that spent time in it) I already had lucid objectives with which I defined myself on arriving in the household. My abilities regarding the household's religion thus quickly extended to also include an enhanced understanding of how to employ the religion not only as a survival instrument but also of how to easily use it sometimes to get even papa over when no one foresaw its being possible. That singular understanding may demonstrate how I could succeed not only in the household but also in situations where many people similarly placed just would not be able to figure a way out, like surviving as a moneyless foreign student in North America, Canada precisely.

19

Papa practised another religion called farming or handwork. I intensely remember him telling us on several occasions that schooling is good but that it is best when backed by handwork. Yes, indeed, many of us might not have seen the validity of his thesis then but I can vouch for papa's farsighted and larger picture view. If you could profess this religion well, you were always welcomed to the household. It was so much a religion that papa would certainly have refused his transfer and probably resigned if he were sent to a city like Tokyo or New York where he could not find a farm to buy and cultivate. This part of the Chapter harps on the importance of this 'religion' to staying and progressing in the household in particular but in life generally; first doing so through my father's transfers and my own forest and farm experience, before cementing with (1) three uncles that I would call *nyanga* man, yard boy, and driver, (2) the market day revolution and the learning capacity of some of the children of the household.

The Job Transfers and Farming/Forest Experience

Papa's job transfers and farming could exquisitely account for why I seem to have a fortune with *many* (of almost everything). For instance, most people go through primary school attending just one school but I attended at least three; also passing through three different secondary and high schools. Most live all their life in one city and country but I can scarcely give an accurate number of cities I have dwelled in, in three different countries and in two continents. These transfers and farming could also partially account for my somewhat 'unstable' love life in the early stages of my primary schooling; but these transfers would here illustrate how firmly implanted the farming 'religion' had become; so too would be my own forest and farm experience, including my unique understanding of how to easily get even papa on my side using the religion (discussed under the Market Day Revolution).

My father was being constantly transferred to different towns and he always had farms in every city he lived in; but Yoke was actually

20

the Farm Capital. On the second day of school in Catholic School, New Town (Victoria, Cameroon) we were rushed out because papa had been transferred to Yoke. I therefore spent less than two days in that school. Attending Presbyterian School Yoke until class three (second term unfinished), my father was again transferred to Kumba, still in the South West Region. I was enrolled into Sacred Heart School Fiango, Kumba, where I went until class six before papa was sent back to Victoria where I completed my primary education in the same school I had started it in. The transfers kept coming. Papa was even transferred to Douala but he refused, hiding behind his not speaking French; but I think the real reason might have been the belief that he might not find farm land in Douala, if we go by the usual 'over pepper and salt' stories of the "been to" people. We did not also move to Bamenda in the North West Region. As there was no French cover, my father went alone most probably because he found the cost of moving the entire family (with close to fourteen children then) from Bamenda to the Farm Capital for two weeks work not worthwhile. Realizing he did not move his family to Bamenda as expected, Sonel quickly re-transferred him to Victoria where we had still been officially based while he was gone alone, though practically but in Yoke during all holidays. Most people in the various other cities where we have lived (such as Victoria and Kumba) never really considered us as residents of those towns because as soon as holiday began, we were heading for Yoke in Muyuka the very next day and only came back 'home' about two or three days to resuming school.

If I say that I began working in the forest only in Canada, then I would not only be undermining said religion but also not being truthful about the essential survival training my father gave me. In the forest in Canada – precisely in Dolbeau-Mistassini in northern Québec – when you arrive for the first time, old or experienced workers (the *ancients*) have this tendency to frighten you with bear stories. These stories did not frighten me at all, thanks to papa's handwork. For one thing, our farms were mostly forests when my father bought them. This fact can be clearly seen in the names given

21

to some of the farms. One in Muyuka we called Black Bush and another Monkey Bush (in Yoke). Black Bush got its name because while in it you could hardly see the sky. It was almost as if it was night time in that farm by the time we started clearing and cultivating it. Monkey Bush was due to the great amount of monkeys and others of the same 'family' that would be playing noisily from tree top to tree top while we are tilling the farm. Big Bush (in Yoke) was the largest of the farms; being also noted for the huge amount of reptiles, rat-moles, and tarantulas that inhabited it. And what is more, we worked in those farms that were highly infested with more dangerous forest animals without much personal protective equipment like safety boots, helmets, gloves, etc.; and with cutlasses and hoes, not engine saws.

Some of the *ancients* thus came up to me with their bear tales and were amazed when I cut them short with my own probing: "Would you *ancients* be working in the same forest as *nouveaux* like us?" They said of course. "Can these bears clearly distinguish an *ancient* from a *nouveau?*" They were stunned that I was not falling into their trap and so I continued: "What makes you think then that those bears would only come after me?" They left me alone but I did not let them get away with it. The next morning in the bus that was taking us to the patches I reassured my fellow *nouveaux* with this free lecture (in French, since it was a French-speaking company in northern Québec that is infested with Africans from Burundi and Rwanda):

Listen to me very carefully, guys. Those who see bears or other animals in the forest are those who want to see them. If you get into your patch and just bear in mind that you are there to do your work, the bear will obviously see you since you are actually visiting its place of abode but it will be happy that you are there cleaning it and will just pass by unseen while you are busy with the cleaning. But if you get there and instead of doing your work you go nosing around for a bear, you will certainly see one because it will come to you wondering why you are there and not working – and, with the sighting of a bear, it will be practically hard for you to work on that same patch, at least, not on that same day.

22

My first season with Aménagement MYR Inc. (in Dolbeau-Mistassini, Québec) would also speak volumes not only in regard of the farming experience but also in connection with knowing what I was up to and up against. After about a week or two cutting trees, I was at the centre of the talk of the camp. There were of course other newcomers that equally excelled but my case was outstanding for some reasons. Knowing that I was not only a university graduate with a doctorate degree but also a university lecturer, many had given me just the first day before they were to see me packing and leaving. Even the guy (Alain Tchato) who had taken me along explained later that he did not just know how to refuse (like many had done before him) bringing me along especially as I had been very helpful to him when he had arrived in Canada, not knowing what was in store for him in the country. That he was not at all sure I was going to cope with the task but he would still have done his part by taking me along as I wanted.

My first patch of almost three hectares was between those of two *grands coupeurs* (very experienced tree-cutters) from Cameroon who had patches of almost the same dimension. They had been talking among themselves (in Bamileke that they did not know I somewhat understood) that I was to spend not less than two weeks there after they would have been long gone. As these *grands coupeurs* advanced, they kept looking back to see how far behind they must have left me but realized I was always on their heels. Unbelievable for a newcomer, they later told other West African *grands coupeurs* (Guinea and Mali) who were not present to "*chop* Christmas with their own eyes." The one on my left (the guy that had brought me along) finished on the sixth day and I completed on the seventh day, about an hour before the one on my right whom I aided for those sixty minutes. The news spread around the camp like wild fire.

A lot of the *nouveaux*, because of the frightening stories from the *ancients*, are forced to take to working in pairs (which is usually also a big distraction as most of the day is spent talking to, or checking on, each other). The bulk of those who have actually encountered bears have done so while they were not busy working, or had brought

23

along some foodstuff that attracted their attention. The truth is that most of these stories are narrated by the *ancients* for obvious reasons, the most important being that you will spend most of your time being afraid of bears and by the end of the season (about four to five months) you will badly need to "buy" a lot of patches from them so as to be able to meet the minimum amount required for full unemployment for the non-season months. It is thus a business strategy for the *ancients* and a lecture like the one I gave in the bus does not sit well with them since it lets their potential clients know what they are up against – very unlike many of my nose-poking neighbours of the patches I have had to work on.

These nose-pokers were clearly not able to comprehend how I go about it with so many machine stops and concomitant "schooling" in the forest (doing two jobs in one) and yet did not: first, have accidents and, second, end up at the end of the season "buying patches". It all boils down to knowing yourself and not trying to be someone else. There are many known cases of workers who would not even stop their machines in order to eat a sandwich or an apple simply because they continuously hear the neighbour's machine going almost all-day. They thus behave as if they are in some sort of Tree-Cutting Olympic Game; or that the neighbour would have cut all the vast forest before they could complete their particular patch, if they took a break. And, most often, they end up taking more than just a few minutes break, and not in the forest but in hospital.

Several people do not have more than one "career" in their life but I have had so *many* that I find it hard to sometimes to describe myself with any one of them: Lecturer-in-law; warehouse clerk; tutor; taxi driver; library clerk; writer, office messenger; student; production line worker; author, *débroussailleur;* research assistant; *préposé aux bénéficiares;* farmer; general hand; night watchman; teacher; construction worker; and independent researcher. But none of these 'professions' has provided the most incentive and immediate ingredients for the writing of this book as that of *débroussailleur.* The advantages associated with this job are many but a few stand out. First, there is the freedom; second, the time; and, third, the reflection

24

potentials of the forest. Freedom entails the fact of being practically your own boss, deciding when and how to work without, for instance, the *yala-yala* yelling from supervisors and other heads associated with factory and other jobs in town; all this deriving from the forest remuneration style that is based on piece-work rather than time-work. By time I am not just referring to the off-season months but as well to the ability to create or take time off work and do something else (such as developing an idea that has struck you, or to just relax) without having to ask permission from anyone.

As I told one of my primary school acquaintances in Kumba, I have what some would call a magnetic brain. But I could very vividly remember most of the things that took place many decades ago not only on that score. I have found the forest to be an ideal place for reflection and development of my own proper ideas. And this began since working on the farms in Yoke, the Farm Capital. The sole difference being that in the Yoke case there is too much room for interruption of thought since we work very close together unlike the other forest where (but for the machine noise) you might not even realize that you are not alone there. While working in the forest in Canada for the second and third seasons (the first season having been solely for focusing on sufficiently grasping the techniques of the job), I was able to relive, in a unique way, the events in my head, grasping all the details of some of the conversations and facts herein included; all these happening while the tree-cutting was going on – thanks enormously to the separation and balance/cooperation skill developed long ago in my Kumba primary school. I sometimes stopped the machine just to be able to jot down the details before they could vanish by way of ceding place to more behind them waiting for their turn to resurface. All these occurring thanks to my quick grasping and positive employment of papa's "handwork" – very unlike many of my father's relations that flocked to the household but could either not profess its religion (like the *nyanga* man and yard boy) or did it so profusely well and yet could not be 'ordained' as expected (like the driver).

The Nyanga Man, Yard Boy, and Driver

I am sure papa got his farming practice and philosophy from his own father, Fon ST Fossungu. This fact can be picked up from Aunty Tumekong who babysat me. She was very proud of me when I was leaving the village because it is often said there that if the child you babysit is going places you also are going places. She had come the day before to say goodbye and one of her pieces of advice to me was:

My junior brother, you are very lucky because your chances of studying without interruption are great. Do not play with that. We here in the village cannot study in that way because of farm work over which the Fon does not joke. He is right though because, without the coffee, how could he be able to send so many of us to school? Please, don't forget all what I have been telling you over the years.

Aunty Tumekong was right (although quite wrong about farming practice and philosophy in *ncheng*, like most of those rushing to the household?) because while still in the palace, I used to witness a lot of what the Fon did to any of the farm-going age children he found at home while others were on the coffee farms, such as the *nyanga* man and mates.

The Nyanga Man and Yard Boy

There are usually a lot of children in the palaces that some Fons do not have an idea of the exact number; but not my grandpa. He not only knew every child by name, he also knew who it was, from their voices; including grandchildren like me – Ateh-Afac. In the village that is the way one is called, not by the first name like Peter (except to distinguish from another Ateh-Afac) and never by the family name, Fossungu, that usually designates the Fon. I vividly recall this incident when a group of four big boys were at home rather than on the farms and heard grandpa coming. Three of them managed to escape, one being badly caught by grandpa's baton. The fourth, Uncle Joseph Efemlefo Fossungu (later Chief Fosanoh), had thought he was very sage by quickly climbing on and hiding in the barn. To his

26

surprise, grandpa stood at the door and yelled: "Efemlefo, come down and get your punishment. I have always known that you have nothing in that coconut of yours you call head; otherwise, you will not be acting like the stupid rat that ran into a bottle to escape from the cat. Come down by yourself or I'll bring you down myself, animal!" Before showing himself up, grandpa must have listened for a while to them talking and laughing and thus knew (without even seeing them) who and how many they were.

Father Joe (for that is the way Uncle Efemlefo insisted on being called by us when he came to live in the household in Yoke) was clearly not the farm type but more of the showbiz guy. Back from the farm (when he went at all), he would spend so much time bathing – to scrub off anything that has to do with the farm from his body, he would often justify. The time thereafter in front of the mirror dressing in complete white (did he really want to be a priest or father?) would be about thrice as long, with him taking many and different *posteurs* as he went about it and also self-congratulating the other guy in the mirror at every new positional style taken. When all that would be over, spanning some hours, it would then be time for the sprinting walk around in order to select the best moves for the evening. Where Father Joe used to dress up like that to go to, no one else really knew. In short, it was therefore not long before Father Joe relocated to Douala (Cameroon's Toronto or Hollywood) because he was a confirmed *nyanga man* or what the French call *viveur* and clearly had no place in a household where the farming that he despised so much was such a religion. Neither could there be a place in it for someone with the 'tree-top' mentality like the yard boy.

Uncle Linus Anamoh Fossungu (henceforth Uncle Anamoh) studied in National High School in Kumba and came to live with us in Yoke. He was so full of himself and evidently lazy, by the religion's definition. I would say he is in the class of people that put their pride in front of their reasoning. I say this because when you let what you want to accomplish in life define you, and not what you do for a living, you will quickly understand that it is not what you do in life that gives you your worth. Once you know your worth, you will do

27

whatever you need to do to move on in life and realise your goals. This realization perhaps explains why I seem to have a destiny with *many*, including professions and academic qualifications. The shrimp's or *njanga*'s reasoning that belies all these numerous professions would obviously be unacceptable to anyone who finds his or her worth only in the type of job he or she does. For example, papa secured Uncle Anamoh a job in Powercam as a yard boy but my uncle saw this as insulting for a secondary school graduate like himself who should instead be working in an office. He exchanged bitter words with papa and thereafter very angrily left the household. Of course, if papa was like the others, he could have used his position in Powercam to secure the so-called office job that my uncle wanted, but I am sure yard boy was the available advertised job; and that papa wanted Uncle Anamoh to get in and earn his position by himself through climbing through the echelon. You clearly get this impression from papa's description of Uncle Anamoh as someone who "wants to be on the top of the tree without climbing through its trunk." I will illustrate this prophecy further with an event in 1985.

Papa was very upright and endowed with wisdom that sometimes bordered wit and prophetic sarcasm. For example, in 1985, he had a ghastly (motor-cycle/car) accident in Victoria on his way to work, an occurrence that almost ended his life. Madam Catherine who was then his *njumba* or mistress (he later married her officially) came from Yoke to take care of him in the Victoria General Hospital where he had been almost abandoned to die. Meanwhile, his wife, Mami Thecla, was busy mocking and telling Madam Catherine that she was working for nothing (as my mother put it, *monkey dey work bamboo dey chop*) because she (Mami Thecla) had all the keys to the cupboards and documents and would be the one to access the money and properties when papa will die. Learning of this when he had miraculously recovered consciousness, papa wondered if my mother had already read *The Book of Life and Death* to know that he would die before her. As if he was prophesising, my mother died in April 1998, about four years before my father.

28

Papa could also have been prophetically right about Uncle Anamoh because this uncle later attempted running a university-like institution called CADA (Cameroon Academy of Design and Arts) without capital. I am not very sure I still get the full name of the Academy right but the acronym was rightly CADA. The sweetest talker of the entire Fossungu royal family, Uncle Anamoh recruited young college graduates who worked round the clock for him without pay and sleeping on hard floors, always believing in his sweet assurances that money and the good days were just a stone-throw away and coming faster than they could imagine. He almost succeeded, as the story goes, in giving away a lot of the Fossungu clan to *nyongo* (a money-giving, human-eating cult) in his bid to acquire his capital, the one last thing that was then lacking to have CADA go fully operational. I am sure Uncle Anamoh (like many others that lived in the household) did not quite know what gives him his worth. If he did, he would have used his natural ability to talk papa into helping him out with the money at that stage. Could this possibility have crossed his mind but his having ruptured links with papa stood stiffly in the way?

Most probably, it is, because papa is that kind of person that would always spring back to help anyone who has proven him wrong or confirmed that he or she can do a thing on his or her own. My whole life would exemplify the point; but a very banal example would make the case right here that papa makes errors like every human being; but if you understand him and do not get bitter with him, he will very openly admit his mistake and make amends. No one practically taught me how to ride a bicycle or motorcycle, not even how to drive a car. I did all those by myself, from merely intelligently watching others doing them. Papa had this habit of always attending 'First Mass' on Sunday. While he took his bath and prepared, I was charged with getting his Suzuki out and cleaning it, even as it was seldom dirty. I usually did so fast enough and went riding for a while and getting back before he came out to go. One day I miscalculated my ride and by the time I was back he had waited for quite a while. Evidently crossed, he stated that he who had bought the motorcycle

29

had not even mastered it as much as I seemed to have. "Now my question to you is: Tell me when you will buy yours! When and how are you going to purchase yours? Is this not how you children of today start thinking of getting into money-getting cults?" But some months later there was a medical emergency requiring rushing to the pharmacy in the main town of Muyuka and, taxis being as irregular as they are in Yoke, I made speedy use of the Suzuki and saved the day. "P," papa immediately admitted when I returned, "I was wrong indeed for scolding you for having learnt how to ride this machine so well. Good Gracious! Just see what would otherwise have happened!"

Uncle Anamoh's problem then could be that his pride ruled his reason rather than the other way round; thus the story of his "mortgaging" people in the family to *nyongo*, with Uncle Ntimah and wife being top of the list as Uncle Anamoh's father and mother, respectively. When Uncle Ngufor was told that he too was part of the list, he merely laughed and retorted: "Since when did wizards and witches begin to eat bitter meat?" He was obviously alluding to the story or belief that *nyongo* does not accept a person you offer them unless you and that person are close enough and see eye to eye; which was clearly the contrary between these two uncles of mine, both of whom lived in the household at different times and towns – Uncle Anamoh first in Yoke before Uncle Ngufor in Kumba.

Uncle Anamoh obviously did not like Therese (my senior sister) for the nickname she had given him. In Yoke papa was one of two workers that had the company's phones at home and he had the habit of calling home from work to give some instructions from to time to time. With the multiple arrivals of many uncles and aunts, the status of Bangwa in the household obviously changed (as compared to when I had arrived in the household in Victoria) since most of the newly arrived – although also speaking "good English" – held the mother tongue in high esteem. And since they constituted the majority by then and proudly used Bangwa, those of the household that did not speak and understand it found themselves at a disadvantage and earnestly began seeking to at least understand it, in order (as it is often said in Nwangong) "not to be sold in their own

30

presence". One of papa's calls came and it was Uncle Anamoh that picked up the home phone and papa demanded in Bangwa to know who it was and he said "Me" (*meng*). You who, papa asked and he again said "Me." Papa was obviously very crossed when he shrieked "You Who?" to which Uncle Anamoh responded: "Me, me, Fo [Chief] Linus." Hence, Therese who was then present gave his nickname in Bangwa, *Meng-Meng Folinus*. Meng-Meng Folinus was very unlike the driver who practised the religion of the household extremely well but could still not be ordained as largely expected.

The Driver

Arriving in our household (like several others) in search of greener pastures, Uncle Ngufor was very hard-working especially on the farm. His stay was much longer than most others' because, as I said earlier, if anyone can practise the religion of our household as well as Uncle Ngufor, his or her staying power is enhanced, notwithstanding the invited *Big Mami Trouble* (to be explained shortly); since in this case the negative forces would concentrate on working against your progress and not your presence. Exceptionally intelligent and generous, Uncle Ngufor could not go beyond primary school simply because of similar home conditions in his senior brother's home in Fontem (South West Region). He was not the birth child of Fonenge's wife, the madam of the house, who must have had similar fears and distrust of him as did my mother of me. It seems to be most mothers' trait, judging also from the way my own birth mother must have treated my half-siblings. I was not there in Nwangong with them but could gather this from the way Mami Regina, first, never even mentioned them to me and, second, categorically refused to stay with Esther and Awandem in Ekona, as I had arranged in 2004 when I visited Cameroon. The whole idea behind the arrangement was to regroup the family and make it easier for my guidance and help (as head of the family), and also in catching up with the lost years of scattered living. But Mami Regina would be willing to stay with my girlfriend's family in Bafut near Bamenda in

31

2007 and with the family of Uncle Calistus Tenangmock Fossungu in Douala since 2008. As you can see, it is not just Mami Thecla who is in this *not-my-birth-children* pot. But if you are wondering a lot why mothers generally behave that way, then wait until you meet an African-Canadian 'mother' (in a later chapter) who does not even see children (birth or not) as being part of her own definition of family.

Uncle Ngufor was the only relation that showed insatiable interest in the academic progress of the children of the household as well as in his own self-growth. He was very gifted and I say this for a lot of reasons, a few of which are stated here. First, I remember how he (not having been to secondary school) used to write to me while I was in Sasse College. Whenever I got his letters my friends and I would have to gather around with our dictionaries to be able to comprehend his language (the style and big terms he used) as well as marvel at the beauty of his handwriting. Sasse College, it must be noted, is like the Harvard or Oxford of colleges in Cameroon. Second, I do not know when and where Uncle Ngufor ever took French classes to be able to not only communicate in but also write French perfectly. I guess that must have been the edge he had with easily picking up the driver and do-all job with the Nigerian businessman, owner of Ets. Echo Automobile in Douala and Kumba, after the disillusionment he got from papa.

I am very positive this uncle would have been an ideal mentor to all of us had he been sent to college; having gotten to the household in the early 1970s while we were in Kumba, with all of us still in primary school. All this uncle was given was the opportunity to learn driving, which he embraced with an open and grateful mind. I kind of "knew" a lot about the art of driving at that time and age without having formally learned it because Uncle Richard is the kind that loves to spread his knowledge around through demonstrations and recitations; and this even during my days in the village. He excelled in his driving course and graduated as one of the tops in his batch and was the one nut every taxi owner and other transporters in town were looking for. But he preferred and stuck to papa's promise of buying him a car of his own. The materialization of that promise took so long but Uncle Ngufor was patient, working as hard as ever alone in Yoke while we were in school, with us only joining him during holidays. His friends from the driving school who were then plying the Kumba-Victoria road (that cuts through Yoke-Muyuka) would sometimes recognize him on the road behind a well loaded truck of farm products and stop for a while to ask him why he was wasting his time on the farm in Yoke when he should instead be doing what they were doing. After the wait for several years and numerous missed opportunities out there, the bombshell fell one day when my father announced to Uncle Ngufor that an old land rover car had been bought for him at an auction by Sonel (papa's company).

One other thing I admired so much in Uncle Ngufor is his frankness and outspokenness, which are evidenced also by what we mockingly referred to as the *Muyuka High Court System*. When we moved from the Yoke Powercam camp to Kumba and came back to work on the farms in Yoke and Muyuka during holidays, we used to stay in Muyuka at my mother's parents' home in Strangers Quarter. It became habitual on Friday evenings for my mother, mother's mother, and mother's grandmother (The Prosecution) to put us, one by one, in front of The Judge (papa), demanding for punishment (without defence) for any minute or irrelevant thing that we might have done during the week. It was truly a harrowing exercise to both Accused and the Judge. Imagine papa, for instance, having left work that evening, rode his Suzuki all the way from Kumba (or Victoria) to Muyuka (about 50 kilometres, but double or triple it because of the nature of the road and papa's go-it-slowly way of riding). Instead of resting on arrival, papa would sit there for hours on end 'judging' this and that until sometime past midnight, then continue his ride to Yoke where he would barely have slept before it was morning and time to be on the farm all day. All this must have led papa to find a way to put an end to it by redesigning his house in Yoke after the bar that was being operated there closed. We thereafter started staying there instead, when we came for farm work, thus avoiding the *Muyuka High Court System* thing.

As one of the notorious accused (Akana and I being the others) in the *Muyuka High Court System*, Uncle Ngufor, in always insisting on and actually defending us and himself, might have been inviting more than *Big Mami Trouble* for himself. I actually coined *Big Mami Trouble* from the Muyuka High Court System because of the following factors. When it initially began (before Uncle Ngufor's arrival), Akana and I had tried explaining to the Judge that what the Prosecution was saying was not correct. (And they used to actually inflate or invent the charges a lot.) Papa's question then was often "Are you Angel Gabriel to think that I would take your word against those of three people?" Stunning, isn't it? My head went to work, turning this over, applying the arithmetic that I then mastered, and came out with this: If the Judge should one day realize that I am not an angel, let alone Gabriel, and decide to look for the mean of the Prosecution (Mami +Big Mami + Big Big Mami), he would still end up with Big Mami, which was, of course, still a lot of trouble in the *Muyuka High Court System*; hence, *Big Mami Trouble*. Was Uncle Ngufor conversant with the *Big Mami Trouble* concept but simply ignored it because of his headiness when it comes to doing things the way they ought to be done?

Whatever the case, he also did not mince his words regarding the Land Rover Affair. He told papa there and then he was going to have nothing to do with that land rover vehicle because it was not an auctioned car papa should have bought in the first place; that the vehicle was surely going to turn him into an evil person and put a strain on their good relationship since it was to be a regular patient to the hospital called garage. As later events showed, Uncle Ngufor was right; and papa himself even celebrated when he eventually practically gave that car away for free. Having thus realized his error, papa went into a business deal with him some years later, culminating in the purchase of a bus for transportation; all this because reasoning, not fighting and bitterness, was the tool Uncle Ngufor employed – the same strategy I later also used in the market day revolution – a revolution that was badly needed to get a working-day off the household's religion.

The Market Day Revolution and Children's Learning Capacity

Papa's "handwork" was such a creed in our house that only Sunday (put aside for the other widely known religion) provided the only day off in the week during holidays. Farming was sacred in our household so much so that if there was anything you wanted from papa and you were not sure to get him on your side, it was better to wait until after a good day's work on the farm. He loved hard work not only in school but as well at home and on the farm. I guess my fulfilling all three spheres could be regarded as my "magic portion" for progressing in the household against all the odds. But even the camel needs a drink of water in the waterless desert to be able to get the load on its back across the same. There came a time I, for one, actually wanted a day off the week. Wednesday is the Yoke Market Day and was the target. The Market Day Revolution had to take place.

None of my brothers and sisters thought the day-off thing would ever work with dad (who was so feared by them). I told them to just watch me as I make the 'fight-less' revolution. As already noted, my father worked in Victoria (now called Limbe) but he always came up to Yoke on Friday night, riding on his motor-cycle, to farm on Saturday before returning on Sunday. One Saturday then, after a hard day's chores on the farm, I explained to him during our 'food break' right there on the farm that we needed to be having the market day off so as to aid our mother with cooking and other market exigencies. Moreover, I added, Wednesday is in the middle of the work week and a perfect day on which to rest and be reinvigorated for the three remaining farming days. Papa did not particularly like the idea but he could not also see how to condemn it (especially as it was proposed right there on the farm, with the day's heavy half-day output still very much lightening up his heart), so he put it in the hands of our mother. "Tee" (for that is the way he called his wife, Thecla), "what do you think about Peter's suggestion?" Obviously, papa was hoping my mother would say she did not need the help. My siblings were amazed that it had even received this reaction, not outright rejection;

35

but I knew it had already won. Obviously, my mother was deeply in love with her drinking and this proposal provided her with more time to be with it. The revolution had been successful especially because reasoning rather than fear was the leader.

There is also a foreman in the forest where I worked that almost everyone says is "racist" and the like. It happens that people are sometimes just afraid of others and have to find a reason to attach to their unfounded fear. Pascal Perron (the foreman) is simply strict like papa and many black Africans always see strict people (that they cannot corrupt or bend around at will) as wicked and, because Pascal is white, they rush to equate his strictness with racism. Because of this inhibition in their minds, it is thus hard for them to engage Pascal in any fruitful discourse. For example, one time we began working in an area where the bus does not reach and we had to be transported from the bus terminus to the patches by pick-up trucks. The first day I watched Pascal transporting five persons, with the folded sixth place near him unused; and with a lot of the Francophone African workers voluntarily hanging in the baggage compartment of the truck (this is even not allowed by regulation). The second day was the same story. On the third day, as Pascal was about going, I called out from inside the bus for him to wait. He stopped and I came out of the bus and reminded him that there was an empty place near him that I wanted to occupy. To everyone's surprise, he smiled so broadly, removed his GPS and other belongings and unfolded the seat for me to occupy. From the fourth day on, that seat was never again empty and it is not like Peter was the one always occupying it, even as it had been quickly nicknamed 'Peter's Seat'.

Fear inhibits learning and dialogue. I could not have gotten papa or Pascal over if I partook in the fear of him as the others. My first nickname in the household is *Peter-Tekam-Uhm* (PTU), a nickname that taught me a lot about women, learning, and the difference between fear and respect. The PTU nickname was nothing to me; it was the beatings that traumatized me and they began almost as soon as I had set feet in the household. Akana (my namesake's son) had

36

especially conferred upon himself the right to hit hard on my head that I almost became dumb to avoid ever uttering a sound in their detested Bangwa language. But I guess several positive things resulted from that. First and foremost, it sent a quick message to my brain that it had better be fast in learning. It paid off as my head began ticking almost around the clock; a fact that could be responsible for explaining most of the other many nicknames that I later bore (such as Mr. English, Mr. First in Class, Pythagoras, Lord Denning, Power, Figaro Cinq, Professor, etc – some of which will be seen later). It also paid off in the sense that, although I started school on the same day with both Joseph and Akana, Joseph (for instance) obtained his secondary school diploma the same year I obtained my high school diploma and his high school diploma three years after mine.

It aided me furthermore– and this is the biggest gain– to establish some sort of direct line with papa whose nickname (that I did not understand) is indicative of the way he was feared in the household. This fear of papa is clearly seen in the nickname that the older children particularly employed to signal to each other his presence or arrival. Papa's nickname, *EN*, is actually his first and middle names abbreviated. I initially never understood the signal, not speaking 'their' language then and often being 'caught' by the tiger (as they thought); fortifying the story of my own first nickname. Unaware of the *EN* signal that sent the others into hiding, I often was the one papa 'caught'. This 'catching' coupled well with my always remembering my birth mother's last advice to me before I left the village, namely, that no matter how much I was disciplined (beaten) by papa I should always "run and enter only between his legs" (literal translation from Bangwa, which means running into his house and never to somewhere else) because "he is the only father you now have". So, I was thinking, if I must only run to papa when he beats me, there is even more reason to go to him when someone else beats me up the way Akana and the others were doing.

Therefore, I usually profited at such times that I was 'caught' to find out from papa (in Bangwa that he enjoyed speaking with me) why the others were treating me the way they were doing. Papa would often reassure me that they meant no harm and were just helping me to learn the English language as fast as I could and be able to go to school. Bingo! Go to school? Me? So I could also one day demonstrate and sing "One Summer Day I Went By" like Uncle Ngufor used to sing to us in the village whenever he returned from Fontem where he was then living and schooling? Was my ignorance (of the fear-instilling *EN* signal) not being a kind of virtue here? Was Uncle Sam Fonge not visionary in insisting that I speak only English, not pidgin as the others? The day before departure from the village Uncle Fonge had also been at my birth mother's to say goodbye, leaving me with this advice: "I hear there is some funny way of talking in *ncheng* and I don't want you to come back here talking that way. Speak only English and I would be very proud that my nephew went to *ncheng*. Do you understand me?" My birth mother had corrected him for thinking that he needed to emphasize for me to comprehend.

I did not then quite understand both of them because I had been preoccupied with reconciling Uncle Fonge's stress on my speaking only English when I am in *ncheng* with Mami Thecla's insistence on my English name. After the three straight days spent at Mami Cecilia's at Mami Thecla's request, I had gotten to our compound (that is off the palace but a stone-throw from it) without being aware of all the people that had greeted me on the way or those that were behind me; this because I was lost in thought, still puzzling over some of the questions I had been asked by Mami Thecla during those three days. For example, to what is your name, I had said "Ateh-Afac"; and she had indicated that she was talking about "your English name". I had searched hard because I had so many names various people called me with but was then not sure which of them could be "my English name". For instance, grandpa used only Ateh-Afac; my birth mother called me by two names – 'Ateh-Afac' and 'Fonwancheng'; and Aunty Tumekong who babysat me used 'Fonwancheng' and 'Mbinchang'. Which of these names was English? I was thinking hard; suddenly I had thought of my namesake Fonwancheng whose names before he became chief of Nwancheng quarter in Nwangong were Peter Ateh-Afac and I had then shouted: "Peter." All this had taken quite some time, more than anyone who knows his or her name needs; and if my questioner had been trying to assure herself that I was not as sharp as she must have heard, then she must have been satisfied to the brim.

Here was I then in *ncheng* and what was I hearing? Is pidgin what Uncle Fonge was referring to as a funny way of talking? What was going on with this only-English thing? And what was I to do to quickly learn the 'school-going' language? As previously indicated, I don't know how long I probably lived in Church Street in Victoria before beginning school. All I know for sure then is that Therese's schooling had abruptly ended in Victoria long before mine began; and that I entered primary school the same day in September 1968 with both Joseph and Akana. I don't know for precisely how long Akana had been living there before I arrived but I know that on the very first day the three of us got to Catholic School New Town, Victoria, he was immediately promoted to the next class because he was just too big and old for a class one pupil. On the second day our schooling was cut short because papa had been transferred to Powercam Yoke where a bully was transformed.

A Bully's Transformation and the Pepper Incident

In Presbyterian School Yoke I soon became known as Mr. English, thanks to the influences of my first teacher, Miss Mandengue. Sam's Mother openly used this Mr. English reputation as a successful wakeup call to her son. Sam was this boy in the Powercam camp who liked bullying others (including policing his senior sister) and had been looking for every opportunity to do same to me, but to no avail as I had initially been engrossed by Miss Mandengue at school and almost completely ignored children and their activities in the camp. Then in and winning in a big way, I went to their house one day and when Sam was rudely asking why I was there and saying he would beat me, his mother was not amused. "Empty head Sam," she wanted to know, just how are you ever going

39

to beat Mr. English with your pidgin? Pocket your petty jealousy and know that if you learn to carry the bag of someone that is more than you, you can gain a lot from him. The only way you could beat Mr. English is not only to be as gentlemanly as him but also to do very well in school, even if you are not exactly Mr. First in Class like him. And don't you ever go about asking him again what he has come here for because I, the only one that should be asking such questions, do not see anything wrong with your senior sister associating with a brilliant gentleman like Mr. English. Do you hear me?

Sam's Mother was one real icon I had in the Yoke camp because of the way she always spoke her mind on issues, no matter how controversial others found them and either kept quiet or talked from both sides of their mouths. I think this is one of the major problems (if not the most devastating) facing Africa generally but Francophone Africa in particular. Take the Therese Pepper Incident for instance to demonstrate. Therese was six years older than me and died in 2012. She was papa's first child from a previous marriage. Her mother (as the story goes) had attempted to poison papa at the instigation of her *njumba*, a Nigerian man. I still shiver till date reliving Therese being tied up naked by Akana and Uncle Anamoh in the presence of my mother and father and most of the children of the Powercam camp in Yoke. They then introduced ground pepper into her private parts; all this happening simply because of accusations of her having slept with a man. Apart from Aunty Tumekong from our household, Sam's Mother is the lone outside voice that came out strong and swinging in condemning it. It was very shocking to Aunty Tumekong (who is about the same age as Therese) that she left the household almost immediately and settled in Douala. Whatever Therese might have done with a man, she clearly did not merit being treated that way. Doing this to her, not even behind papa's back, seemed to indicate that papa had extended his problem with his first wife to the child of that failed union; especially as he thereafter personally took Therese to the village and dumped her there, the idea being for her to stay there permanently and rot. Was papa really someone who treated his children without bias? Therese's "pepper ordeal" indicated two

40

things very clearly to me; namely, first, Mami Thecla's make-or-destroy powers in the household and, second, its resulting from the accusation of having sex, certainly sent an always present cautionary message to my head as to the way I was to go about this boyfriend-girlfriend business. Going to Sam's house that day had nothing to do with her senior sister as he was thinking.

Sam's Mother having finished with chiding him, welcomed me and offered me something to eat and was back to what she had been doing with her daughter in the kitchen. This time she seemed to have also hammered down the truth nail into Sam's psyche. They say truth is bitter and hurts but that does not mean it must not be thrown at someone's face like she had done to Sam's here. Sam was kind of paralyzed by it because, in addition to "embarrassing" him in front of his rival, his mother had also openly opened the door to his senior sister's heart, ushering me in if that was what I wanted. His sister had momentarily come to say hello and returned to the kitchen.

Sam was still saying nothing but I noticed that he was no longer looking bully-like and started conversation. "Sammy Boy," I began and he seemed to blush, certainly because of my calling him 'boy', and I added jokingly "Or should I say Mr. Bully?" He now got the message clearly and simply said "Thank you for coming here today." I understood him but wanted him to explain himself further so I said I did not quite comprehend what he was driving at. At this time both his mother and sister were there, hardly believing that they had heard Sam well. He turned to his mother and said "Mom, I am sure I would not have seen reason if you were not the one throwing all these things at me. Thank you for making me to see my real self." To the sister, Sam apologised for his past behaviour towards her, a thing that was, according to him, now in the past. Turning back to me, Sam wanted to know if I would be his friend now that he has found himself. I extended my hand, saying "Sammy, you have always been and will always be my friend; but if you are talking about a renewal or reinvigoration of that companionship, I have no problem with that." You could actually touch and feel the joyful disbelief when Sam turned to the others with "Did you hear English from Mr. English?

41

Mother, you were right and I wonder why I had not been seeing what I am now seeing in him." Sam and I became real friends and shared a lot of things in attempt to both compete and cooperate with each other; all this happening thanks to Sam's Mother's comprehension that, bitter as it is, people must be made to confront the truth head on. Only this can help them and thus ameliorate things for more and more people. Just imagine the number of people that no longer suffered from Sam's bullying and you would have seen how that works; and this in the same way as strong and powerful arguments – something missed by most of my siblings largely because of the infamous definition of family.

Missed Learning Opportunities

In the household I had quickly learnt that most people like papa are not hostile against you as such but against some comportment or trait that you may be exhibiting. Once you can realize this and do your best to take away that trait or behaviour, the hostility goes with it. The fear that is consequent on the hostility also vanishes and both of you start relating in a very productive and mutually beneficial way. The advice I would like to give to most parents like my father is that they have to learn to be strict without appearing hostile; because not all children with the ability to learn can go beyond the hostility to do so. Because this elimination of the object of hostility had not been done by most of us in our household (again, most probably because of the exclusionist categorization of family and children), the fear of papa developed to a point where even my mother was afraid to inform him, for instance, that the monthly or weekly *chop moni* (food money) was depleted or nearing exhaustion; always preferring that I be the one to tell him. They thus were seeing me as papa's favourite, with lots of their own trouble for me attached therefore.

The distrust of me in the household was further enhanced by the fact that I understood papa to the extent of even knowing, for example, when any of us was in for trouble, just from the way he called for that person. And I usually told them they were in trouble

42

before they actually got to him to find out that I had been right (and they sometimes even accused me of being the cause of their nuisance: otherwise, how did I know?). That is how some would hastily jump to say I "have four eyes" when it is that simple. My father seldom used our full names unless he was crossed for something you had done. So when he called out 'Peter!' I knew there was trouble; otherwise, I will hear 'P!'; the same going with Vin, Joe, Ben, Marie, Bea, Anna, Mo, (no trouble); but Vincent, Joseph, Bernard, Marie-Claire, Beatrice, Annastasia, Maureen (big trouble).

Akana stood the greatest chance to cooperate with and learn from me but he seemed to have been so contented with being the hangman of the household, totally oblivious of why his father, my namesake, must have sent him there in the first place. Self-esteem was clearly at the centre of Akana's failure to grasp a lot of things. For example, who else but such a person would be ashamed of wearing his uniform and carrying his own school bag or blackboard to school? Furthermore, Akana forgot to bear in mind that I was in a sense his father and therefore that a father may know certain things more than the son. When I had explained the logic of the Muyuka High Court System to Vincent, indicating that it was better to go in for *Big Mami Trouble* without the aggravating circumstances that Uncle Ngufor's insistence on defence was inviting, he had beamed and said "Eh, Mbi!" Mbi here is the short form for Mbinchang; and this was the very first time I heard Akana calling me anything out of *Peter-Tekam-Uhm, Big Head*, and *Short Thing*. I had then begun thinking that maybe he had finally realized himself (like Sam) but that was only my thinking because (as Sam's Mother would put it) bullies do not think; they just bully.

I recall also telling Akana one day (when he called me *Short Thing*) what I had heard from Sam's Mother. I was telling him this in the hope of making him think and thereby displacing Sam's Mother's thesis. But that only called for more 'shortening' cracks on my head, thus validating the thesis instead. Thinking aloud, Sam's Mother had wondered if "this intelligent boy will ever grow an inch taller with all these cracking from Vincent Akana and the heavy loads he is often

43

made to carry." She was obviously right about the loads, until the advent of the farm truck; but I do not know if her height postulations can find some backing in the fact that all my three blood siblings (Awandem, Esther, and Dieudonné) are quite tall. The experts in the field can occupy themselves with that while I concentrate on the children in the household.

Before I left the village Akana's father had come to say goodbye and impart advice as was traditional with anyone even remotely connected to me. Conveying several messages to his son, Fonwancheng had specifically implored me "to make sure to take good care of your son, Vincent Akana; give him the necessary advice so that his stay in *ncheng* is worthwhile. I use to worry somewhat but now that you are also going there to be with him I am happy and reassured that everything will be fine with him. Don't forget that he is your first son." Imagine then the enthusiasm with which I had first encountered Akana, addressing him as "my son" while passing over his messages from my namesake, his father. It is obvious that my employment of those two words (my son) had completely thrown him overboard, begetting the hostility that he thereafter wantonly exhibited in my regard. This was clearly uncalled for, for anyone who has his or her self-esteem. There are children in the village named after my birth father who, to date, refer to me as their son, always wanting to know what their child has brought them, whenever I visit Cameroon. It is only normal. Moreover, being a village-born like me, Akana (unlike the coast children of the household) should have been the one to better appreciate my situation when I had arrived and to give me the required support for 'soft landing'. On the contrary, he championed the onslaught of the trauma that paradoxically aided me not to partake in their fear of papa that prevented them from dialoguing or reasoning with him on issues.

There was much potential for my siblings *of* the household to pick up a lot from me, especially the girls (who were all born while I was already there and) who always called me 'Brother'. But it seems they were soon prohibited from too much association with the "outsider". To concretely illustrate, there was this tendency for them

44

to answer "Sir" when papa called. One day I sat Maureen down and inquired from her why she addressed her father 'sir' instead of papa. She did not seem to see the importance of the baffling question but said it was the way everyone else answered him. I asked her if that 'everyone' included me, and then she remembered and admitted that I always used "papa". I then asked her which of the two was more appropriate. Before I could even complete the question Maureen was all thanks for the eye-opener. As soon as she began responding "papa" when called, everyone else followed suit and it became the norm at home and quickly spread out to other households in the quarter. Imagine for yourself the future of these children if the definition of family was different in the household.

As for the two young boys of the household, they also did well in school in some sort of competition with me, which I found good and progressive. Like Marie-Claire, Bernard also made it to university graduation and beyond. Joseph especially, for some exclusionist reasons, did not take advantage of my presence in the household; otherwise, how else would you explain his being barred from entering the University of Yaoundé because of his lack of Ordinary Level English (not to even talk of mathematics and French) when he grew up in the same home with Mr. English? Most often when Joe wanted to know anything from me at all it related to how to *cockler* a girl. *Cockler* was generally used in the community but I heard it for the first time from Joseph who had a nag for creating his own words or phrases and for giving people nicknames from nowhere. I remember asking him how he came about the word and he described it to me: You know how a cock does when it wants to mate? I got it right away because for the first time I saw *cock* in the word. I never got to know how Joseph came about *ekapulapong* that he often employed to demand where others, have put their brains. He would for instance ask a sister who has done something wrong whether she has any *ekapulapong* in her head. The term is now generally used, especially in Yoke.

John Azimbe, nicknamed *Money Hard*, was then also living with us. I do not know the exact nature of the relation but John's father

45

seemed to have been either papa's maternal cousin or uncle. They were living in Yoke in papa's house, part of which someone was using to operate the only bar then in town. When we moved to the Powercam camp from Victoria, John started visiting, then staying the night sometimes, and finally became part of the household, an act that was duly ratified by his moving to Kumba with us when papa was transferred there.

Hardworking on the farm as well, John's main problem was that of not admitting that he had a long hand even when he has been caught red-handed. In the household we always ate to our full but John was never getting enough as far as rice goes. He had this habit of always sneaking back to the pot and scratching rice off as if a rat or something else did it. Akana wanted to solve this rat-and-no-rat mystery and set himself to work. He caught John in the act but the latter was still denying; this, coupling with John's way of always swelling and murmuring things when Akana was beating him up, earned him Akana's incessant wrath. The latter interpreted the former's comportment as challenging him and the more he beat the more the swelling and murmuring, and the more the beating. I once advised John Money Hard to learn to take his punishment without provoking the hangman but he would not listen to advice; instead counter-suggesting that we both team up to beat Akana up. I asked him if he reasoned with his head or with his anus. Akana was a bully for sure but I cannot enumerate how many times Money Hard himself unnecessarily called for trouble from the bully. Akana was a real bulldozer on the farm and after returning from it, he often dozed off and slept so deeply, snoring heavily and with mouth partly open. John would on many occasions put some large amount of salt in his mouth and then make some very loud noises that would get him up. You can imagine the rest of the scene.

John was a very good footballer and surely would have gone places with it had he reached class seven or even college in the household. Around class three or four, he absconded when we went to Yoke for holidays, never coming back to Kumba with us as usual; preferring to remain there, doing his sand work. The altercation with

46

Akana is largely the cause of John's leaving the household despite that (unlike other "outsiders") he had all the chances of smoothly progressing there. For example, as he was not a Fossungu, he was not regarded as any threat; again, he was younger than Joseph in age and school standing; and generally not as attached to the household as I was. When we usually came down for holidays he stayed with his parents in Yoke and not with us in Muyuka (as was the case at the time of the *Muyuka High Court System*). I suspect his mother did not give him the kind of advice my birth mother gave me; but I think all largely depended on John knowing who he was and what he was up against, things he did not seem to know when, because of Akana, he refused to return with us to Kumba, where my goals were palpably threatened by the stiff challenges in CCAS (Cameroon College of Arts and Sciences) where the short-cut to university education was effectively hatched.

Chapter 2

University Education, With Or Without Money: The Fight For And In Cameroon College Of Arts And Sciences (CCAS) Kumba

This chapter examines the fight for and in CCAS Kumba, while the next two look at the elongation of the short-cut to university; both processes being, of course, the result of the exclusionist definition of family and of child. Solomon Enomah Tatah (Solo), a bosom friend, who once described me as 'a man of many' must have done his homework well because I have *many* of almost everything, including fans and nicknames. One of my many fans, Solo is the one who coined the *Power* nickname. The General Certificate of Education (G.C.E.) Advanced Level is normally acquired in Cameroon after two years in high school but I obtained it in 1981 after 'less than one year' in CCAS Kumba. Three years after this academic accomplishment, I met and knew Solo in the University of Yaoundé (UNIYAO). First excitedly introducing himself to me, Solo lengthily narrated his elated experiences when he actually got to first see me in November 1981 in CCAS Kumba (after having heard so much about me and even read some of my test scripts that had then become standard materials for the high school's G.C.E. hopefuls), including the commotion and admiration my arrival there had caused.

Solo was right. At the time in Douala and still uncertain of my academic future (as you will see in the next chapter), I had learnt that I had some money to claim in CCAS Kumba in connection with high school entrance performance. I got there only to realize that I was the talk of the day, with some of the newly arrived students like Solo then having the chance to actually meet me, their hero and mentor. It was undeniably nothing short of a star meeting his or her fans. Coupling this with what also took place at the UNIYAO, Solo had then concluded that only a very powerful person like he thought I was could accomplish such feats; and, therefore, *Power* was the only name that, in his estimation, befitted me.

Solo and I just happened to have been renting in the same *mini-cité* (student residential apartment) in Ngoa-Ékéllé, the quarter in Yaoundé where the UNIYAO is located. But listening to Solo and the way he articulated both his points and his English told me a lot about him and we immediately clicked in. Very frank, open and a fire-brand straight talker, Solo is the kind of person you can easily learn a lot from even while cracking jokes. I particularly commit to memory this joke he started one day regarding my not respecting the UNIYAO tradition of few or no *mentions* (honours) by obtaining so *many*, always having one in all the examinations I took there. This accomplishment, Solo thought, was quite unusual especially for an English-speaking in the vastly mono-cultural and French-speaking UNIYAO.[5] I then playfully but seriously explained to Solo that tradition is made (for better or for worse) by someone like me; so I do not see why I cannot then also be making tradition by doing what I do. If many more people should start doing it the way I do then a new *mention*-having tradition would be here to stay, which, by the way, I concluded, is the way a society evolves. Solo then also insisted on the fact that I was 'a man of many'. And, truly, it was largely thanks to being 'a man of many' (disciplines) that the CCAS challenges failed to put an abrupt end to my destiny with many.

The Challenges of CCAS

CCAS Kumba must have been considered by the opposing forces to be the furthest I could ever go, crowned especially with an unsuccessful completion of its programme of study. This was surely the end of the end, as they did happily muse about. Although I excelled in both, when I went to CCAS Kumba, I was a student more of sciences than of arts. A day student for the first time, I was living

---

[5] For more on the vexatious issues Solo is raising here, seeFossungu (2013a).

in a room in our house in Bamileke Street in Fiango and attending school in CCAS situated on Buea Road. It is by all means not a walking distance; and not also a one-drop taxi affair (the taxi concept in Cameroon and most of Francophone Africa not being the same as in the West). Because of this new student-life style, I actually began better appreciating the fact that I had not been admitted to a government *lycée* after my go-getting performance in the Common Entrance and First School Leaving Certificate, and thus ended up in Sasse College where the lump sum payment of one's school fees would include everything (like sets of uniforms, and books) so that whatever one was given as 'pocket allowance' was in fact just pocket allowance.

While in CCAS, my allowance for each term (three months) was ten thousand francs CFA, with the popular justification being that I did not have rents to pay. But the many imponderables far outweighed the rents that I was not paying. Some required laboratory equipment, for instance, cost about fourteen thousand francs CFA. Was I ever going to make it as a science student without the necessary study tools? Was this not the certification of failure that some forces (both inside and outside the household) had for so long been ardently working for? Was I to capitulate and let them have easy victory? What were all these unannounced visits to Kumba by papa for? For the answer of the make-or-die questions, I drew very heavily from my first teacher who meant the world to me then – Miss Mandengue. I had to say yes to not persisting in beating competitors over her to avoid dismissal from the snake-beating male teachers that were hovering all around her. But this time in CCAS, NO was the answer to capitulating because I badly needed to obtain the G.C.E. Advanced Level which I saw then as a sort of window to the world and the success that Miss Mandengue herself had predicted for me. I never got her overwhelming love but from her lap-lecture I got something so precious that none of the snake-beating teachers could ever come near to taking away from me. I had therefore to step up the fight that began with (1) the CCAS admission itself as well as (2) some other earlier educational admissions.

51

The CCAS Admission

The almost intractable financial and associated problems in CCAS were not the beginning of the battle because even getting admitted into CCAS Kumba had been a lone and personal fight. High school education seemed to have been put beyond my reach when the list of admitted students to Cameroon College of Arts, Sciences and Technology (CCAST) Bambili (in North West Region) had come out without my name on it, despite my having nine Ordinary Level papers with good grades. The forces I was up against had seen this as the clean and clear end of the road. I was shocked but kept my calm. When you define yourself through objectives such as I have, you tend to look at the larger picture of things. For example, if I am telling my story to (the world generally but) my wife and children particularly, it is not to gain their pity or sympathy. It is principally, if they learn to look at the larger picture, to let them be able to correctly appreciate not only who they are and who they have as husband/father, but also to be pleased about all those who have shaped my life in one way or the other. In that way, they could better value my mother (Mami Thecla), because, without her role, I am not sure I would be married but to their mother and that they (as they are) would actually be the ones I call children today.

As a larger picture person, you thus move from small ideas to big ones; not the reverse; you tend to pioneer bigger things and to easily surmount obstacles that are on your way to becoming better; most often being guided by the knowledge that panicking at every obstacle does not help. You thus confront narrow-mindedness with progressiveness, not with the same; because, otherwise, you never can advance. What I was confronting before and in CCAS Kumba was obviously the handiwork of small minds and I understood that meeting small-mindedness with small-mindedness could not lead me anywhere further.

The next day (following the CCAST list), therefore, I quietly went up to Buea (the capital of South West Region) to put my case before the regional (then provincial) delegate of education (by a presidential decree of 2008, the ten provinces of the country are now known as regions). As fate would have it, that same day the principal of CCAS Kumba was right there at the delegation compiling his own list of admitted candidates and the delegate quickly sent me directly to him. (Just imagine that I had panicked after the CCAST list and stayed crying uselessly in my small room or packed and left the household like Marie-Claire wanted to.) The CCAS principal was very impressed with my results (of course I was not receiving the high-school-entrance money mentioned earlier for nothing) but had one small preoccupation, namely, why I had not chosen his college (but CCAST) as first choice. I had to quickly improvise and explained that I had been ill at the time of filling the forms and my friends had made the choice for me, knowing that I was more a sciences student than an arts one (what a beautiful lie!). The CCAS principal told me there and then that he was admitting me to his college but that I would not have a place in the dormitory. I thanked him, reassuring him he would never regret his decision.

The CCAS Kumba fight obviously taught me so much about obtaining not only academic admissions but many other things on my own, which would all be tied to the description of "a man of many". The main academic problem has been the financial means (and/or the bribery requirement, for Cameroon). Take admissions into study programmes of universities. Most persons consider themselves extremely lucky to be admitted to a study programme in a university. I easily had it with the following: *Docteur en Droit(LL.D.)*, January 1997 to December 2000 @ Université de Montréal, Montréal, Québec, Canada; Master of Laws **(LL.M.)** (Air & Space), September 1995 to February 1997 @ McGill University, Montréal, Québec, Canada; Master of Laws(LL.M.), September 1991 to November 1992 @ University of Alberta, Edmonton, Alberta, Canada; *Diplôme d'Études Approfondies(D.E.A.)*, October 1988 to September 1989, *Maîtrise en Droit*, October 1987 to September 1988, and *Licence en Droit*, September 1984 to July 1987, these three being @ Université de Yaoundé, Yaoundé, Région du Centre, Cameroun.

The foregoing are those that I actually enrolled in, completed and obtained the degrees and certificates; but they are not all because also worthy are: Master in Public Administration (MPA): admitted July 1999 @ School of Public Administration, Dalhousie University, Halifax, Nova Scotia, Canada; Master of Arts (Public Policy and Public Administration): admitted August 1997 @ Concordia University, Montréal, Canada; Magister Juris in International Law: admitted July 1995 @ University of Malta, Msida, Malta; Master of Philosophy (M.Phil.) in Criminology: admitted February 1995 @ The Institute of Criminology, Cambridge University, Cambridge, United Kingdom; *Maîtrise en Droit de la Santé:* admitted August 1992 @ Université de Sherbrooke, Sherbrooke, Québec, Canada; Master of Arts in Personnel Administration/Industrial Relations: admitted July 1992 @ Graduate School of Industrial Relations, Saint Francis College, Loreto, Pennsylvania, USA; and Master of Business Administration in International Management: admitted March 1991 @ The Centre for Management Studies, European University, Montreux, Switzerland. While the CCAS battle prepared me well for other academic battles ahead, its own success cannot be dissociated from (1) earlier admissions struggles and (2) the short-cut decision to leap from lower sixth form to university.

The Other Earlier Educational Admissions

The daunting challenges for and in CCAS would be appreciated through looking at similar earlier events that had groomed me well for victory in CCAS. I will thus be examining admissions (1) from primary school to college and (2) from Sasse College to World Wide Missions Secondary School (WWMSS) Mpundu, Muyuka. I passed out of primary school in high-flying colours but my high-powered performance did not secure me a place in a government Lycée "due to the very corrupt demeanours of [especially public] school administrators" (Fossungu, 2013a: 183). Not being admitted like this has become normal in Cameroon when you don't go through the back door. Very upright in a time and place where most people

54

regard crookedness as the rule, this 'back door' business is something papa would never do or countenance; and the proof is with Uncle Anamoh's bid for an office job that, as you already know, ended woefully. This non-admission also was supposed to be the stop point to secondary education. But unlike my tree-top uncle, I had therefore personally 'climbed through tree trunk' by finding the way to Sasse College all by myself for the college's own interview. The small private "messages" from Mami Regina were aiding very significantly. It was then that I really understood her insistence when I had told her not to worry sending these "messages" to me but concentrate more on Dieudonné with them. She had said she could not listen to me on that score, stressing that if I thought I did not need her "messages" I still had to accept them from her "and then perhaps pass them on to any beggar at the side of the road, if you like." What a mother!

The crooked nature of the country's public school system thus landed me in one of the most prestigious Harvard-like secondary schools, Sasse College. I remember the then Sasse College principal (Reverend Stumpel) expressing shock that, with the kind of results he had before him, I was not admitted in a government college; also telling me there and then that I was already a student in his college. What I consider as really sending me to Sasse (quite apart from Mami Regina's timely "messages") is the fact that admissions lists to all their colleges were always posted in all the Catholic Mission churches around the country. My name conspicuously featuring on those lists (Sasse's for that matter) was just too much of an embarrassment if I was thereafter actually not attending Sasse College. After four years in single-sex Sasse College my destiny with *many* refused to be put aside for secondary schools.

The Sasse College admission did not end my pre-CCAS admissions woes. The Sasse College administration had dismissed our entire class during third term in 1979 and required re-application through coming together with father. That was to have been the end of my secondary education and, therefore, the end of the academic road for me because, for one thing, papa was never going to go with me to Sasse College for whatever reason. He did not do so for the initial admission and it was not now that he was to do so. The class dismissal was even looked upon in the household as if I was the only one involved, not "the entire class as he is trying to fool us with." Second, I do not know how others (without "four eyes") saw it but to me the then African and non-reverend principal (known to us as Pa Ngando) was a bully-like one. I have my way of not giving bullies the chance to exercise their calling on me; and this because I know that fear (a one-way street) is not the same thing as respect which is a reciprocal affair. Anyone who grew up with my father and did not fear him would scarcely fear other people especially when it comes to reasoning with them. I will draw few examples from across my various professions to buttress the Sasse palaver.

I was then one of the *Chargés des Travaux Dirigés* (Graduate Teaching Assistants) at the UNIYAO. This is precisely 1990 I am talking about. We had this problem of not being paid for the work we were doing and we went to see the dean about it. The Faculty of Laws and Economics Dean (Professor Paul-Gérard Pougoué) began threatening us, saying that we were lucky to have been given that favour, with a monthly amount of sixty thousand francs CFA; and that if we continued joking around (by making our demands) the favour would be withdrawn, etc. The few of my Francophone colleagues that had even ventured into the dean's office (a lot of them could not even come near it) had already vanished when he had begun his menace. I just could not swallow all the unnecessary lies and threats and had to cut the dean short with my own lecture to him (to the consternation of the few colleagues and the dean himself):

Mr. Dean, with all due respect, first, I do not see the favour you are talking about; second, you do not have to threaten us and think that will resolve the problem of our unpaid services; third, you talk of the monthly sixty thousand francs *bourse* as if that is the payment for our services as *Chargés des T.D.*, pretending to forget that every *doctorat* student (whether *Chargés des T.D.* or not) is entitled to that monthly *bourse*; and, fourth (I do not know about the others but), if you think

56

the *Chargés de T.D.* thing is a favour, then I am demanding that my name be taken off it right away.

By the time I had finished saying all this (in French, since I wanted it to sink well into his skull) everyone still in the dean's office was fixated because no one had been expecting anything of the sort. I had to remind the dean (after some minutes of his saying nothing) that I was done with what I had to say. It was then that he got out of his absorption and said: "I will look into your problem, thank you." When we left the office and met the others anxiously waiting, Francophone colleagues who were present explained it to the others: "That Anglo is something else: you need to have seen the way he was talking to the Dean, not at all afraid, and actually giving him a lecture that the dean who was very menacing at first ended up comprehending very well. The problem will obviously be solved." It was by acclamation that the group then made me their spokesperson.

I have had similar encounters with managers and supervisors where I have had to work in Montréal (Canada), notably, Lockwood Manufacturing Limited and Rossy Dolarama Inc. Most of these people confound fear with respect. The latter, as I have said, is a two-way street. They tend to have this feeling that everyone should be shivering when they come around and if they find that you do not behave as such, they jump to say you are disrespectful. And when I then give them my usual true and bold lecture, they often go nuts. In the case of Rossy Dollarama, the manager's going nuts got to a point where I actually threatened to take the manager and the company to court for racial profiling and the upper echelon of the company had to step in to quell things.

Perhaps the Sasse College principal must have interpreted my fear-free comportment wrongly (just as the supervisors and managers in the course of my many professions that confused fear with respect); placing me on the blacklist of ring-leaders of a class action that was clearly spontaneous and leaderless. Viewing the entire situation from the perspective of a larger picture person, the double jeopardy in going back to Sasse College (with or without my father) was unmistakeable. But I had a year of college to complete and

57

complete it must be. This is where the religion of the household (farming) has been a very handy tool to both sides – to the dismay of the other side that (like those confounding fear for respect) saw only the one-way of it. It was because I was not bitter and was still there in Yoke practising the religion during school period that the unexpected occurred. This is also where not getting bitter as a result of being open-minded was serviceable.

Looking at the larger picture of things can be, first, a device to avoid despair and move on; second, a means of achieving what you set out to accomplish; and, third, a way of correctly analysing a situation to appreciate what the alternative event would have meant, just as my analysis of the double-jeopardy in the Sasse re-application; all of them being linked to one another, of course. Farming (especially alone as I was then doing) has always been an invaluable occasion for serious thoughts for me. I had already concluded on the farm that I was going to sit for the G.C.E. Ordinary Level as an external candidate; but let us get back to the narration of the unexpected mentioned earlier that put out the external candidate thing – my very cordial relationship with my then nauseating sister Josephine and especially her husband (Monsieur Philippe Kamdom, the college teacher and our tenant who had impregnated her) and his brother, Monsieur Jean, who owned the only Francophone professional college in Yoke.

The school proprietor, my *moyo* or in-law, was surprised to find me in Yoke farming at a time when I was supposed to be in school in Sasse and I narrated the story to him. It was therefore Monsieur Jean who kindly took me to see "my Bamileke brother" (his words), who was then the WWMSS-Mpundu principal, for a place in form five in his college. I got the place there despite that I did not return to Sasse College to re-apply and write the third term examination to pass to form five; my first and second term report cards being convincing enough. Monsieur Jean was thus very helpful and I remember telling both principals, when everything was done, that "you both have just made history by doing what you have just done"; and Monsieur Jean whom I did not know knew me as much telling the WWMSS

58

principal (in French) that "if my school had an English-speaking section, I would not have brought him to you because I know he will bring you and your school a lot of publicity with his performance." Monsieur Jean was certainly correct and I did not fail him. All these past academic admissions struggles then came flashing back as I was thinking of what the next move in CCAS Kumba will be that would not also fail the principal of CCAS as well as me and Miss Mandengue. The first and persistent thing that presented itself was the idea of "a man of many" forgetting about aeroplanes and medicine and leaping from lower sixth to university by switching to arts.

From Sciences to Arts: The Great Leap to University Education?

It was about three weeks to first term examinations when I had decided that I was spending only one year under the unbearably tough conditions in Kumba; conditions that could not be justified in any conceivable way other than the sure certification of failure. It is not like my father was poor and financially unable to carter for me there. He did more than that while I was in Sasse College for four years. Papa was very rich but preferred to live simple, investing a lot in houses, farms, and his *birth*-children's education and future. I am very certain that any of his children who wanted and was willing to (like I was), could have gone to any university in the world without any money problems. For instance, in 1985 he single-handedly sent his first son, Joseph, to the United States of America for undergraduate studies and beyond. It was thus clearly not the issue of lack of means as that of the forces opposing my advance solely because I do not come within their definition of family and of child. I quite remember that the defining conversation with papa (noted in Chapter 1) took place in Kumba when I was in class five. I recall having talked about it to a Kumba primary school acquaintance who "really want[ed] to meet that father of yours who must surely have passed on his whole head to you." Here then was I in CCAS Kumba, about eight years later, trying to be better than my father by advancing academically so as to better help the greatest number of persons possible; and being tied down by papa himself? Surely not him that I must have to thank in the only manner he likes; which means not agreeing just to eschew discord.

Not Agreeing Just to Avoid Disagreement

To solve the problem being forced upon me in CCAS (and thus thank papa like he never ever imagined), I requested a switch to arts from the head of department and the vice-principal. Granting this simple request was not quick in coming because the sciences department head thought he could convince me to stay on, even wondering aloud to me: "If guys like you, with five Ordinary Level science subjects among nine are leaving to arts, who are those to stay in science?" That was a very poignant question that would have easily swayed anyone that was just trying to follow the breeze without any sense of direction or purpose. Until this time, it had become almost instinctive for me to say NO to or resist anything that meant NO to my academic progress. I would use an illustration here which also makes NO an answer to any attempt to make me capitulate from what I believe in, as well as hinging on the somewhat "typical" African family definition and/or roles.

As a graduate student and research assistant at the University of Alberta, we went to the Kananaski resort in 1992 for a graduate seminar weekend together with other graduate students from other Canadian universities in Manitoba, Saskatchewan and British Columbia. It was looking very promising and hectic. In total there were five African students (Blacks) in the lot, three Nigerian guys with me from Alberta and one Ghanaian lady from Manitoba, I think. The first evening the film shown for discussion touched delicately on racism; we all watched and thereafter the discussion began. Participants said whatever they felt like saying about Black people, with the five of us there and participating and following the

60

dialogue without losing our composure. Remember we are graduate students from Africa, most of us very ripe and more than mature.

The second day the film and topic were on the sexes or what some would refer to as feminism, with the film depicting a man battering a woman; the root cause of the altercation being who was to do the dishes. You would not imagine enough just how red most of the female participants had become even before discussing the film had taken off. Emotions were really running high and a lot of the male participants were finding it awkward to even say what was on their minds. The ladies had obviously taken it too personal and I was truly amused at their charging when I took the floor to contribute to the issue. I prefaced my contribution with the fact that I was actually surprised to be witnessing the kinds of emotions that were being brought into an academic discussion as this; the redness growing with every word that was coming out of my mouth. But that was no reason to shut me off and an utter war was considered declared when I pursued: "Where I come from there would not even have been a problem at all because there the majority of women would even get very angry just finding their men in the kitchen, let alone doing the dishes...." I do not think I even finished the sentence because hell had broken loose with sonorous calls from the feminists for me to apologize before the class could continue. Retaking the floor after the noise had died down, with everyone waiting for the infamous apology, I stated very clearly and loudly: "When we are mature enough to continue we shall continue; but, if an 'apology' from me (for what?), is what is necessary to continue, then we had better begin packing our bags and heading back to our various destination because, as far as I am concerned, there is absolutely nothing to be apologizing for." That is precisely how the four-day seminar ended on the second day, despite the all-night behind-the-stage attempts from the coordinator (who was from my university) to get me to "just apologize so that we can move on."

While the Ghanaian woman had openly denied that there was any iota of truth in what I had said,[6] the Nigerian men were very pleased with my performance but kept worrying about how we were to ever get back to Edmonton since they were not sure Cathy (the White lady who had travelled with the four of us in her station wagon) was going to still ride with us. I told them to grow up and/or follow me. Spotting Cathy, I inquired if she had changed her mind on travelling back with us because "my friends here were worried."She was kind of surprised that there was such worrying and simply enjoined: "Why wouldn't I want to return with you guys? I have learnt a lot about Africa just during this trip; and you Peter, what do you intend doing after you graduate?" I caught on the chance to crack jokes with all the ladies she was with by stating that "I might be tempted to stay on if any of you beautiful ladies here has enough habitable space in your heart that could conveniently accommodate me and my bitter truth." Meant solely as a joke, this response seemed to have opened the floodgate and I was almost inundated later by the fast rushing waters; almost similar to the rush to declare me their spokesperson after the encounter in 1990 with the UNIYAO Dean. The message is clear. People who succeed are those who not only know themselves but also have a good grasp of what they are up against in attaining their goals. Such persons do not just follow the wind but chart their own path, even against the storm. Thus, when the sciences department head had finally realized how adamant I was, he let go of me when the first term was just two weeks to go and I went into the inquisition in arts.

The Drama in the Inquisition in Arts

When I arrived in the arts department, its own head tried to make a mockery of me in his English literature class – the first I was

---

[6] For further discussion of some recent attempts or fights by the women and other interest groups for sex equality in government and in public life in Cameroon, for instance, see Fossungu (2013a: 115-121).

attending in that department. The head of department started by announcing that some losers like me think that the arts department is a dumping ground for those who cannot make it in science. Everybody laughed and booed. Next, he demanded the secondary school I was from and I said World Wide Missions Secondary School Mpundu, Muyuka. The booing went even louder and by the time it died down he stated aloud that he knew I must be having four miserable papers at Ordinary Level. I knew it was my time to throw the ball back hard at him and I said absolutely wrong, sir. Everyone was now quiet and he asked "How many then?" I held them in suspense for a while before saying: "Nine, sir; and, if you want to add the Religious Studies from London, say ten." There was stark disbelief in the faces that someone from Mpundu had those results.

Yes, people often attach so much or so little to the name of an institution or affiliation than to the product itself. This attitude can also be seen in how many academic journals have often accepted my manuscripts but later refuse publishing them on learning (from the footnote material they thereafter request for inclusion on author) that I am not currently affiliated to any university institution. They just do not seem to believe that someone "unaffiliated" could have produced manuscripts of such quality. Educators already have the number of miserable G.C.E. papers they associate with certain academic institutions, clearly failing to grasp with Nelson Mandela (as quoted in Fossungu, 2013a: 176) that "It is what we make out of what we have, not what we are given, that separates one person from another." The students in the CCAS class from Sasse College then began claiming that I was not a product of Mpundu but of Sasse and went into the chorus of "Figaro Cinq, Figaro Cinq", with a later CCAS chorus being "read this classic paper", "read this classic paper."

Figaro Cinq, 'Read this Classic Paper' and the Blessing of the
Football Field Mishap

How Figaro Five became like my first and surnames could be a
whole book of its own, but I will try to summarize it here. To begin
with, it is not quite clear which is first and which surname, especially
as in Cameroon there is just no order in the order of names (see
Fossungu, 1998b). In Sasse College the general trend was for the
person to be identified more with the surname that was placed first.
Thus, we would there say Fogam Edwin Khebila, Ayah Paul Takha,
Tabot John Enow (popularly known as Bucaro), Arreyngang Walters
Bullivant, Anusiem Celestine, Fonjock Cornelius Ekenya, Ejuba
Wilson, Kalu Oscar Embola, Nanji Henry Sako, etc. In this book that
cuts across continents, I have preferred to use the Western name
format of First, Middle (where applicable), and Family; an
arrangement still defied by "Figaro Cinq". The story of the first name
would come before the most interesting story which relates to the
'surname' that is still used by my brother Bernard to date.

Figaro is a show-name I had myself chosen for two reasons:
distinction and camouflage. It had to set me apart from all others
bearing Peter in especially night clubs and football fields, as well as
other social milieus. No "chick" (as we used to refer to girls), for
instance, had to be in any doubt as to who was being talked about.
The name did not only sound good and attention-pulling but also
unique to a unique guy. Remember I was at the time a 'college boy'
and, though in Sasse College, was making a lot of waves especially in
Cameroon Baptist Academy in Muyuka with fellow Sasse College and
Yoke mate, Celestine Anusiem. Imagine my father sitting in a
gathering there and hearing talk of Peter being in Muyuka during the
weekend whereas he never saw me there in Yoke (the Farm Capital);
he would surely want to ascertain by asking if it is "my Peter" that
you are talking about. That would clearly not be the case if the same
people were talking about Figaro who is indeed the same "my Peter".
But Figaro became so popular that the cover behind it was almost

64

instantly blown. How could it have been otherwise when Sasse College friends and others would always come to our household asking not for Peter but for Figaro Cinq?

I seem to have something very special with five. That cannot simply be because I have five children (three handsome boys and two pretty girls);they were not there then even though I always knew I was going to be father to that number of children (although not in the least that they would be from three different mothers – thanks again so much to the definition of family). My batch in Sasse is the 1975 Class, a class like no other I have been part of. It appears as if all the Mr. First in Class from all the 'Anglophone' primary schools in Cameroon converged in Sasse that September 1975 to begin a unique and destined journey together. In this batch it was not unusual for there to be constant clashes of wills such as the Fogam-Ejuba one that set almost the entire class into two opposing camps of the 'Cold War'; with Figaro (backed by his home experience) being one notable exception of people that conspicuously refrained from exhibiting the camp-toeing comportment that ensued; and all this notwithstanding his being Fogam's classmate from the Victoria school as well as his next-bed neighbour in the St. Peter's dormitory.

It was also not uncommon in this class for someone who had been last in class (even without failing) in the first term to fight his way to the first position and vice versa. No one was immutable. In this class of the best no one was able to monopolize any position in examinations except Figaro with the fifth position successively. That is how the Cing got stuck to me in the first place. The five was then confirmed in the soccer pitch. I have always used both hands and legs a hundred per cent until high school although, ironically, I do not swim. I had to drop out of most of these things I am gifted at solely because of the CCAS challenges, occasioned by the definition of family. That is, the shrimp bending its back again to counter adverse and menacing conditions, as I have said. Until then, you could not easily tell the difference between my two written samples, each done with a different hand.

The only position in the soccer field that I have never taken up is that of goalkeeper most probably because, first, it involves more use of the hands than legs; and second, it is very associated with swimming (diving). Anyway, as troublesome to defenders as I was with my double-legged play, I was also one of the few defenders (number five) that often stopped equally double-legged nightmarish attackers like Bucaro and Bibum Mbock (both examples being from the same 1975 batch). Although I excelled in many other positions, I became more and more identified with the number five position; with some French language lovers in class (and probably knowing Figaro to be also the name of a French magazine) turning five quickly into cinq that has since sent the English version to the background. It is thus Figaro Cinq (not Five) that reached the college in Mpundu whose results were in doubt in the department of arts in CCAS – thanks very much to my never losing sight of my objectives; ideals that were largely behind my then being in the Academic Inquisition of the arts department head who grossly mistook me for a loser.

The arts department head, apparently still trying to recover from his puzzlement, then demanded my grades in the A3 combination that I had opted for, beginning with his subject, English literature. I told him I did not take it at the Ordinary Level (since it is either physics or literature, not both) and that, again, gave the class reason to laugh. Anyway, he said, you must have done English language at least; what grade in that? I saved his further questioning by simply stating: "English Language, A; History, B; and Economics, B." I was then welcomed to the class, with most of the girls offering me a seat near them. Barely two weeks in that class, I was placed eighth with an average of 10.48 on 20 in the first term examination; with a gapping leap forward in the second term examination; not having to write the third term since I was taking but the G.C.E. Advanced Levels then. I was looking further than my contemporaries were, which explains why 'Read this Classic Paper' soon became another nickname of mine in CCAS.

When you look at the larger picture, you visualize things more clearly than those looking at the narrow. You also define yourself with what you want to achieve, not what you do for a living. An open-secret ingredient of success is open-mindedness or farsightedness (what some easily brand as 'having four eyes'). For example, in class the teacher has taught, say, Milton's *Paradise Lost* up to chapter two but I have already read the entire book. He sets his questions and while the rest of the class is answering based on knowledge of the first two chapters of the book, I am answering based on knowledge of the whole book. Of course, it is only normal that my script would be outstanding. In CCAS it was a general trend with every subject. It became traditional for teacher after teacher, after distributing marked test scripts, to say to the class regarding my script: "If you want to know what was required of you in this test, read this classic paper."

The same trend continued to and advanced in the UNIYAO where 'read this classic paper' changed into the *Professor* and *Lord Denning* nicknames due to the amount of stuff pouring in so many booklets whereas most of my mates would hardly be able to fill one booklet answering the same questions. The UNIYAO scripts were not only classic but also very lengthy and tight in ideas and flow that they became some students' unique study material. One of my UNIYAO lecturers once commented that but for the fact that he knew me quite well and was actually in the examination hall seeing the booklets being handed to me, one after another, he would have doubted that I had produced those answers only in the hall and within the time allotted for the exam. This unbelievable attitude is also seen in how detractors (that hardly know me well) have attempted in vain to frustrate my advance.

I remember the McGill University LLM programme for especially an occurrence that reminded me a lot about my CCAS Kumba battles. During the first lecture in his course, this lecturer (a holder of an LL.M.) wanted every student to introduce self and what he or she had been doing prior to beginning the programme in McGill. Once this guy knew that I had not only been a lecturer like himself but was actually there for a third master's, he felt threatened (for what reason, I do not know); a thing that went overboard when he further learned that I intended to proceed to the doctoral level. He openly told me that I was "overly ambitious." I did not see anything wrong with being that ambitious until when I (with a series of A's in the others) scored an F in this guy's course which, by the way, was "open book" like all the others. The damage was already done because, by McGill policy, no one with such a grade can find him or herself into their Doctor of Civil Law (DCL) programme. Of course, when you are a larger picture person, you hardly carry all your eggs in one basket. The McGill professor had succeeded in barring me from the institution's DCL but not from the doctoral programme generally; just like my detractors in CCAS Kumba thought they had barred me from excelling (in their limited class examination) by reporting this and that.

My CCAS Kumba second term results (even with the zero on twenty in manual labour) were so dazzling that some of my detractors thought they were bringing me down by reporting to the authorities that I had never been doing manual labour. This was at the beginning of the third term and they were quite right. When I had transferred to arts, I left behind the manual labour patch that had been accorded me in the department of sciences and was never accorded one in arts. I did not worry about asking for one since it was not any part of the G.C.E. that I was preparing for. Their reporting this was simply what Sam's Mother would describe as petty jealousy because I was earning no marks for what I was not doing. But the CCAS vice-principal did look at it that way and ordered that I must take care of clearing half of the school's football field; providing my name to every tutor, with firm instructions for them to only allow me into their classes on provision of a note from him. The detractors were very happy that this misfortune had befallen me, saying "we shall see how he will perform as well in the next term examination now that he has been barred from attending classes until half of the field is cleared." They were even doubly happy when they checked every day and found that I was not on the field clearing it.

Unknown to them, however, this mishap was a very timely blessing to me. In fact, my 'one-term' high-powered success in CCAS

68

seemed to be tied to double blessing. While it clearly limited my actual studying in the CCAS Arts department to just two weeks plus one term, there was a double blessing in the CCAS Football Field Mishap. First, it permitted me to put the finishing touches to my G.C.E. readiness with ease and without the additional distraction of further lectures and class attendances. Second, I had a perfect cover that prevented anyone in CCAS from even surmising that I was writing the G.C.E. since my absence from the class examinations (which CCAS makes sure always coincide with the G.C.E. time-tables to discourage anyone from writing both) was interpreted solely as tied to the fact that I had not yet cleared the half football field. It was a perfect cover and it was not until August 1981 with the airing of the G.C.E results that they knew I had written it. I made it flying very high as usual because, as I will keep emphasizing, your therapy begins with you understanding yourself and situation; and in my case in CCAS that necessary comprehension was backed and fortified by Anna's singular love and understanding. Most of the CCAS girls that were throwing themselves all around for me to no avail just could not comprehend me. The CCAS battle had been won through a shortcut, thanks to Anna (then my wife-to-be); but that for actually acquiring university education would largely be responsible, in an oxymoronic way, for the loss of Anna because it was to take a very surprising turn, meandering through what seemed to be a dangerously elongated and snaking double-segment path.

Chapter 3

The Politics of African Family Hitches Elongating Short-Cut: The Bombshell and the Roaming Days

Half-heartedness on papa's part has always characterized my leaving one-level to another in academic progress; and may largely belie the bombshell success. After obtaining the G.C.E. Advanced Level in the lower sixth form in August 1981, the idea was that of using Wednesday, the Yoke Market Day, to compile my file in view of registering for university studies in the then one and only UNIYAO. Therefore, before he left every Sunday for Limbe, papa would give money for the certification of some of the necessary documentation on the following Wednesday. (It is not like all these documents could not be certified in one-shot.) This happened for two weeks and the file was almost complete, requiring just another week to be ready for the journey to Yaoundé. Like Anna (then my wife-to-be), I was so excited but kept my cool at the same time because I never for one moment forgot what I was up against, especially when it always came to leaving one educational level to the other. The more so because of the manner the news of my success in the Advanced Level had been received in the household in Yoke. As Mami Cecilia(who was then papa's inherited wife and my mother's *mbanya*) wondered about it, "How could such wonderful news be received instead as if some very important person in the family has died?"I was absolutely right; and my correctness will see the dropping of the bomb that would initiate my roaming days that would eventually lead to the Anna-fiasco which itself would worsen the make or break year in Manjo two years later.

One major fault I have found in my father over the years is his over belief in those he has confidence in or in those who claim to know things (the experts) that he thinks he does not know. The confidence-fault of papa has worked both ways for me though. Papa

71

generally treated his children without distinction or bias; which could, for example, explain why I did not know Josephine was not his biological child. Of course, when any of them had won his trust or confidence, it became almost like a sin to the other siblings and my mother. This is because, in such circumstances, papa never stops praising you and referring the others to emulate you. Take food for instance. He often found something to criticize in it, not enough salt, too much pepper, meat cooked too much, etc. When there is nothing to complain about, he would say this to the hearing of everyone: "I know it's Peter who has prepared this food." This type of praising did not only turn me into the household's sole cook but also enlisted my mother's distrust that dominated her whole attitude toward my continued presence and progress *in* the household. It is also because of his confidence in me that I (unlike many others) have been able to even progress in the household until high school notwithstanding the constant tussle with the other forces.

But with this UNIYAO-going inclination, the unfavourable forces in the household realized the battle was tilting away from them and towards my side; and, as is usual that truth is stronger than lies, some cohorts from the outside had to be brought into play to reinforce the lies. The outside legion, as I later learnt, took the form of some of my mother's relations residing in Dschang who went all the way to Limbe (while we were in Yoke farming) to convince papa that it was an uphill task sending a child to the UNIYAO (but not to the USA where Joseph will be going four years later?). Studies at the UNIYAO were tuition-free and enrolled students even were accorded *bourse*(monthly stipend that students called *epsi*[7]). Since the talk of uphill task was coming from Pa Martin (as I hear the man at the centre of it is called), it was simply gospel truth; and papa obviously fell for it.

Hence, the following Sunday (13 September 1981) when papa was about to leave and called for me, I was expecting to get money

---

[7] For more on this *epsi* and its assimilationist design see Fossungu (2013a: 175-192).

for the last set of documents to complete the UNIYAO registration. Instead, what I got from papa was this shocker: "I don't think I can be able to continue with sending you to Yaoundé; I am tired and there is no money. Go and find yourself a job anywhere." With those words from my father, I felt the world crumbling under my feet. Both papa and I knew what he was saying was not true but that was not my main problem. It was the timing that puzzled me a lot. Had I been told this earlier, I would simply have gone down to WWMSS Mpundu, for example, where I had graduated in flying colours a year before and easily secure a teaching position for myself. Cameroon Baptist Academy too was just a walking distance from our house in Yoke. At that point and date (13 September 1981), no school could still have been without a full staff, with the school year often beginning between 10-15 September. I was truly shocked and temporarily confused but refused to be bitter.

I had learnt at a very tender age to depend on myself and never to be bitter even when I am disappointed or failed by those I love. Remember the 'biting up' uncle's slap in Chapter 1. This should have been one of the very first things that should have thrown me into bitterness, if anything had to. I will later narrate my ex-wife's 'take and take and take' attitude in this chapter to discuss the new definition of family and why bitterness is not in my vocabulary; thus making no sense why I should have been bitter when papa who (in our own relationship) has been the only giver told me (the receiver) that he could no longer give. Remember also my conversation with Marie-Claire in chapter 1. Not becoming bitter has proven to be one of my greatest strengths in overcoming adversity in life and moving on. A veritable ingredient of success, it is. Bitterness, for sure, will consume you even before the hardship that you are facing comes around to do so. I am therefore never bitter, only what I say may be bitter (truth is obviously bitter, it is said). I think only those who cannot handle the truth get bitter because if you can handle bitterness, there will be no need for you yourself to become bitter.

And here is a bitter truth I reminded myself of on that 13 September 1981 in the comforting arms of Anna (the woman who is

73

not my wife today, thanks mostly to this bombshell): At this point and level, I sternly told myself, if I fail to advance in, and towards, my objectives, the fault would not be that of papa but solely mine. Second, I must always bear in mind (as I had done till then) that many roads could lead to the destination and do not allow the closing up of one road bar me from getting there. Hence, I must again have to find a way around this particular roadblock. As usual, Anna was more than a 100% in the combat as she told me: "Piero, with you and me together, nothing can stop us. I know it is not going to be easy when you are out there alone; but I also know you know I am always there with you. And this knowledge by itself is both our shield and sword for the victory." What better wife than this would any man ask for?

The following Wednesday Uncle Ngufor was on his way to Kumba from Douala and made the usual stop in Yoke. My siblings were all gone by now from Yoke since school had already started. As you already know Uncle Ngufor too had had his own share of unexpected disappointments, both elsewhere and in our household. He had been very disappointed and left for Douala but was not bitter, which explains why he was always still visiting us (and bringing some Douala goodies along) whenever he had the chance like on that particular Wednesday. I told him about the episode of the Sunday before and he was both shaken and reassuring. He told me he does not make much from his job (which I knew to be quite true) but that he would not mind managing it with me, if coming to stay in Douala with him was the option I had in mind. I was so thankful and felt very blessed to have him. As he emphatically added, "you must have to discuss with or inform papa before leaving." I indicated that papa himself had already made it clear that I could look for a job *anywhere* but Uncle Ngufor still insisted that, no matter what, he must not only find out that I have left after I have left. Good and timely advice indeed.

So the following Saturday (19 September 1981), during our food break on the farm, I informed papa about the discussion I had with Uncle Ngufor and that I was to go with him to Douala the next

Wednesday when he would be returning from Kumba in the evening "to see what is left out there for me." Until this moment my arrangement with my uncle had been kept private. My announcement on the farm then sort of hit so hard because, it seems, no one had figured out that I will ever be able to figure a way out of Yoke, the Farm Capital. I was less interested in the reaction of the other adults, paying more attention to papa instead. He seemed to have been turning a lot of things over in his mind, almost like someone who deeply regrets a decision he has just made but finds that he cannot immediately alter it. I perfectly understood his predicament and knew, like Uncle Ngufor had explained, that he was a very good person that was surrounded by a lot of forces that were unendingly desirous of adulterating his goodness. At last he said, almost sobbing, "Okay." But his mood was different for the rest of the day and, but for the fact that I had to necessarily take full control of my future into my own hands (from then on), I would have told him I had changed my mind.

On 20 September 1981 (Sunday) before he left Yoke for Limbe, papa handed a parcel to me that, at that time, I could only have compared to what was handed by the father to the Prodigal Son before he set out; in the sense that papa must have somewhat been thinking that it was the last time he might be seeing me. But, to me, there was no last time with papa whatsoever, even as my roaming days thus began with the ride to Douala the following Wednesday.

Douala, Garoua, Ngaoundéré, and Yaoundé

Uncle Ngufor drives exquisitely well and the ride to Douala was smooth and enjoyable except that I did not get to see a lot on the way since we left Yoke at about 8 PM. But the myriad of city lights that welcomed us to Douala was something memorable to someone who would only have been hearing of Douala in stories from the "been to" people who often add too much salt and pepper to the whole thing. For instance, the impression has often been given that in Douala there are so many companies and jobs that you do not look

75

for the jobs, with the jobs instead looking for you. Here then was a young man of twenty-one who had been told to go and look for a job anywhere and was just arriving Douala to get those jobs looking for him so that he could then choose the one he most likes. But I cannot even begin to count how many job applications I put in, and the number of companies I personally visited for the purpose. After several months there in vain, I had to move on and the South West Region was the natural place to return to. I had a teaching spree there (National High School in Fiango, Kumba; a typing institute in Kumba Town; Unity Comprehensive College in Ekondo-Titi); always moving on because of my impatience with employers that do not pay me when it is due.

I then travelled to the then North Province (current Adamawa, North, and Extreme North Regions); having become very fearless and not having to think I knew anybody anywhere to go there. The journey up north was not through Yaoundé and by train, as most people usually take going there from Douala or the South West Region. I went north by road, passing through Foumban (West Region), Banyo and Ngaoundéré (Adamawa Region) to Garoua (North Region). This voyage reminded me much of my very first trip in life, out of the village to *ncheng*. As we boarded the same kind of Saviem bus (that I had first seen in Dschang) from Foumban, I was wondering if it was repeating itself all over again. The trip from Nwangong to Victoria had been so tiring not just because it was my first; it was not straight and, looking back, I have the feeling we took more than a week to reach destination; having stopped and stayed in several homes in the Dschang area alone (my mother's mother is Dschang); as well as in Kumba and in Muyuka (at my mother's parents' home). Perhaps the journey was that long not just because it was my first; the one up north was not the first, but equally long and tiring. It could therefore be simply that journeys are often long when they are leading you not only to places you have never before been, but also to the unknown. At every home we had arrived my first and sometimes only question had always been "Where is papa *ncheng*?" I guess it had become my way of finding out if we had reached

76

Victoria. There are many other things I would have liked then to also find out, including this strange dream of flying without wings that became so recurrent in one of those Dschang homes that I could almost no longer regard it as a dream. Maybe all the strange things I witnessed in the Dschang homes were just tied to being out of my comfort zone (the village) for the first time?

I particularly remember being left all alone with the baby at what must have been a motor park in Dschang for endless hours. So many wild thoughts had crossed my mind. Have I been brought out of the village to be abandoned here where I know no one? Only the baby's presence reassured me that come what may Mami Thecla was going to come back. But then what was I to do if the baby started to cry? Of course, I had been taking care of Dieudonné and other younger children in the village but this was a coast (*ncheng*) baby and the caring method could obviously not be identical. For example, could I chew hard food and then transfer to this coast baby's mouth for him to swallow as it was usually done in the village? Are these not the kinds of things Mami Thecla should have been teaching me during the three days at Mami Cecilia's? Was she just hiding and watching to see what I would do to her baby?

As if hearing my thoughts, little Bernard broke out crying so loud that I had almost dropped him from the startle. This *coast* baby in my hands had cried for a long while, with me not knowing what and how to do in order to calm him. A kind-hearted lady came by and, because I did not quite understand the French language through which she was asking questions, searched through one of the luggage and found his feeding bottle. She then asked for the baby and I was afraid to give him to her but did I really have a choice? While she fed the *coast* baby, I was wondering what could have happened and might happen next. I had so many upsetting experiences on that never ending journey to Victoria but this *coast* baby incident was the least tormenting; making me wonder till date if Bernard had actually comprehended what had taken place in Dschang when he adopted (if he did so himself) the *coastman* nickname. This nickname has often made me wonder if little babies hear and understand us more than we do to them. I do not quite know if Joseph also actually gave Bernard the nickname *Coastman* (meaning someone who was born and bred in the city and has never been to the village) or Bernard himself adopted it.

Of course, Joseph was not the only 'nickname giver' in the household. But he was very good at nicknaming people and for creating unique vocabularies and descriptions. I also remember Joseph calling Awandem (my half-brother who once came to live with us in Yoke) *Dakilo*, a nickname which soon became so entrenched that I found myself also using it at times. Awandem is clearly not dark in complexion, being lighter than most of us; making it hard to see how he could even come close to a Darky (a nickname usually reserved for dark-complexioned people). This is very unlike my own *Leaky-Leaky Neck* nickname from Joseph that ties in with some scars on my neck that often send out pus. The two boys usually used this particular nickname chiefly when they wanted to make me really mad; but finding that it often did not produce the intended effect, they once teamed up to beat me up. Recalling my grandpa's famous story about the tiger's hunting tactics of going straight for the prey's immobilizing spot, I successfully landed a demoralizing blow on each of them, not giving any opportunity for both of them to attack at the same time. The nickname itself seemed to have died with that lost battle. Decisively making sure that they lost this particular battle was critical because, otherwise, I would have become another Julie to them, not also being able to defend Julie.

Julie is another clear case of helpful ignorance on my part. I never really understood why Joseph and Bernard were often grossly maltreating this little girl the way they did. Because of the lost battle, I was able to defend her from time to time, not actually realizing exactly what I was doing and inviting upon myself. To me, defending the underdog was just the natural thing to do, especially so when it was a small girl being unnecessarily beaten up by two bigger boys. When Julie had arrived in the household at about ten to twelve (at the most), it is like everyone except me was aware of who she in fact was. To me, she was just another Fossungu 'outsider' that had come, as usual. After so many years growing up in the household, with the constant maltreatment as just described, she "carried belly" in primary school, as the school pupils put it. Only her pregnancy brought the message home to me that Julie Fosungu was the wife of papa, the author of the "belly carrying". It was only then that I fully comprehended why Joseph and Bernard had been doing all what they had been doing to her; and that, in their eyes, I must have been regarded as having taken the wrong side in their fuss with papa's new and young wife. Whatever the case, I do think my ignorance here was very useful because, had I been aware of the facts, perhaps I would not have been valiantly standing between the helpless little girl and her multiple aggressors as I did, for fear of the implications; and who knows what would have become of little Julie in their unrestrained hands? Is this not among some of the positive things that have resulted from my 'negative' *Leaky-Leaky Neck* nickname? Was something positive also going to result from the 'negative' of going to Garoua without knowing anyone there?

God Proposes But Man Disposes: The Garoua Guinness Job

It was terribly hot in Garoua but I was already there. The question was that of where and how to begin. To others, this may be a very difficult issue. Not to me because the decision to even get there is more difficult than that of what to do, being already there. As my desire in life is to better the lives of as many people as possible, I would not bother about the type of job I have to do as long as it helps me achieve my objectives. That is why I have had to pioneer a lot of projects, one of which I will now also use to lead you to how I survived in Garoua, as in many other strange places I have been to. The project to be used here is the Douala-Kilomtre-30 Road that will lead you to the Garoua Guinness job that God directed me there to occupy but man stood in the way.

I had been lecturing at the University of Yaoundé before leaving for further studies in Canada in 1991. When I returned to Cameroon after my studies at the University of Alberta, my idea was to continue lecturing, either at the UNIYAO or any of the others that had been created while I was abroad (University of Buea, University of Douala, University of Dschang, University of Ngaoundéré)[8] thus helping young students toward a better and brighter future. On getting back however those in places of authority thought they could keep me out of the environment, for whatever reasons, only they know. Professor Peter Y. Ntamark, the then head of the English law department of UNIYAO II, kept giving me fruitless and endless appointments in Yaoundé, knowing quite well that I was then based in Douala pending being hired.

During a lot of the resources-draining trips to Yaoundé, I was struck by the way people in the villages between Douala and Édea had to suffer just to get to Douala for basic necessities. There were times that I drove past in the early hours of the morning and found some of them waiting to get a paid ride on trucks transporting wood to Douala. On my way back in the evening I would still see them there. On realizing that the university authorities were just out to play nasty games with my time and resources, therefore, I cut off seeking re-entrance into that milieu and took to the transportation business, concentrating on those villages about forty kilometres from Douala and back. I pioneered that road and today, those people have no more problems getting to Douala and back any time of day or night because there are a lot of other drivers who soon followed in my footsteps.

At the start it was not easy for many of the new drivers who came along because the people (probably as a sign of their enormous gratitude) often refused to board their vehicles, saying they would wait for Peter, no matter how long it took. I had to step in to publicly convince them of the need to travel with whoever was available, making them to properly understand that my idea of coming to their rescue in the first place was to make life better for them, not just to make money – a goal that is better achieved when many more

---

[8]For more on the funny creation of universities in Cameroon, see Fossungu (2013a: 184-192).

vehicles are plying the road. After this intervention things changed for the better for all of us because one or two disgruntled drivers openly made some very revealing confessions. According to them, three of them had teamed up and sent one member to the village to get "something" with which to finish me because they had thought I had used some charm to confuse the bulk of the passengers that were refusing to board their vehicles so that I could be the only one making the money. Just imagine where I would be today if I were that egoistic and narrow-minded: long dead and buried, of course. This particular case has many implications but I would highlight it here as a clear indication that larger picture persons know (unlike Uncle Anamoh) that their worth is not to be found so much in what they do as it is in why they do it.

Becoming better is exactly why I was in hot Garoua where (for some months) I had worked very hard in the seaport during the day and, with nowhere to sleep, spent the nights with night watchmen, taking turns with them while each (including me) sleeps a bit. If only he had objectives with which he defined himself and had begun with the yard boy position in Powercam Yoke, who knows where Uncle Anamoh would be today with his objectives? This uncle of mine would certainly be shocked that, then holder of the G.C.E. Advanced Level, I made quite a bit of money as a *chargeur* (loading and offloading cargo) at the Garoua seaport before stumbling upon a job advertisement by Guinness Cameroun S.A. in Garoua that perfectly fit my profile. I went enthusiastically knocking for the position in Guinness. The then branch manager, Mr. Nsoh (an English-speaking Cameroonian), after examining my credentials, told me categorically that he was not going to give me the job because, as he put it, "You are too good and intelligent to be 'locked up' here in my company; you are the kind we need in the university and beyond because in all my years I have not seen students like you who have made their Advanced Level in lower sixth and I truly do not think I would be doing you and this country any good if I employ you here."

I have never before in all my life felt so dejected hearing a compliment like I did hearing those words of the Guinness manager.

The praise made me wonder why *he was not* actually my father. It made me want to wish that the head of the CCAS Arts Department was right that I was a mediocre student. It made me feel like being very intelligent was an offence. It made me feel like God had directed me to come and fill the position but man was preventing me. If only the manager could have known what having that job meant to me then! I earnestly tried explaining to the manager how I myself wanted so badly to go to the university but that I also badly needed the job to be able to raise enough money to do so. He was very unyielding and, instead of offering me the job, he gave me as much money as could permit me to get to Yaoundé and register at the university, seriously advising me not to waste my talents; and stressing that I would be able to manage things out with the *bourse* that the University then accorded students. I was not very satisfied with his withholding the job from me but still thankful for his help, telling him same and leaving.

I still had a couple of weeks within the UNIYAO registration time so I decided not to return to the Garoua seaport (the Guinness incident had truly rendered the city useless to me) but to instead go down to Ngaoundéré (from where I had to take the night train to Yaoundé), and see if I could find something doing there for the remaining weeks. Every franc was important to me since I did not know what was awaiting me in Yaoundé. In Ngaoundéré, I tried several schools to no avail; also failing to find my cousin, Godfred Fossungu (now Fonenge). It was holiday time and, being a government school teacher, he was not in town; but the search for him led me to Mr. Charles Fonkem, then *Régisseur de Prison de Ngaoundéré*. This Bangwa man is not only good but is also truly blessed with a unique wife who had just given birth to their first child (a baby girl they named Solange) when I got there. I had not known them before then but they not only welcomed me into their home with very open and generous hands but, in addition, treated me like the royal that I obviously am but never felt like till then. I was in fact in the position to stay there as long as I wanted but I had to move on, my life objectives calling hard on me; and I also got the family's moral and financial encouragement to pursue further studies in Yaoundé.

Yaoundé for the First Time: A Nasty Coincidence Coupling with the Train and Bus Tickets from God

When I was dropped off at the Ngaoundéré train station that September evening in 1982, hardly could I have predicted anything unusual that could be waiting for me in Yaoundé, the capital of Cameroon that I was then visiting for the first time. I had never been out of Cameroon till then but had, since leaving Yoke in September 1981 and searching for my future, developed this habit of carrying my bag (that contained just a few jean dresses and all my certificates, academic and others) the way North Americans go about with their backpacks. I got to Yaoundé early next morning. Getting out of the Yaoundé train station that morning, two guys in plain clothes sort of sandwiched me and began asking questions in French. I thought at first these were just people who wanted to be friendly and I also found this a perfect occasion to polish up my classroom French. It all started with a simple *comment ça va* (how are you)? I responded that it was alright, thank you; and what about you? They were fine; but continued questioning: Where I was coming from and where I was going to (in Yaoundé). The first was easy but the second I did not exactly know. At this point there was some kind of discord between the two because one was telling the other "It's not him" with the other insisting "It's him alright".

I knew at this time there was a mix up somewhere but what it was I could not tell. I therefore indicated to them (this time in English) that it was my first time coming there and I was going to see a brother, Michael (remember my mother's brother I met in the household when I came from the village?) who was then attending university but that I did not know where in Yaoundé he was living. The guy who had insisted I was the one cried out to his partner (in French): "You see? I told you he was the one. Have you not just heard his American English?" Frankly, until I entered the UNIYAO

83

in 1984 (where and when the language corruption began[9]), even English speakers (my classmates and others) often found it hard to follow when I spoke. Quite apart from being Mr. English in primary school, I was also lucky to have had mostly Europeans as language teachers at secondary level; they tended to encourage rather than chastise me when I sometimes baffled even them in the language. I was known in college to read *The Oxford English Dictionary* the same way other students would read a novel or story. It is therefore not surprising that an African French-speaker should listen to me speaking English and concludes that I am (African) American; but his colleague was still not convinced until what happened after the next query.

If I truly did not know where my so-called brother lives, they demanded, how was I going to find him then? I knew quite well at this point that I was in trouble for being a suspected American spy but I also discerned that lying could not take me very far out because it is extremely hard to be consistent in lies – a very useful lesson that many have not learnt. For instance, my ex-wife is the very one who went about telling people how useless I am to her and the two children I have with her; doing absolutely nothing for them. But she had soon forgotten this when she called the same people to talk about the monthly child support that "was helping me a lot." I was not there but know this because an astonished listener of hers called me to express her admiration that I had been doing all this and yet had been painted as worthless. I simply told Lysly Ayah that it is a good thing that she got both contradictory versions from the same source.

It could indeed be true, as Fossungu(2013b: 104) theorizes, that "Someone who has deliberately taken up confusing and manipulating others as [her or] his profession would often (if not always) end up [her or] himself gravely confused."I do not like talking a lot about the divorce because I like to move on in life by leaving negative occurrences behind me. But since this book is about the definition of

---

[9]For more on the corruption techniques, see Fossungu (2013a: 48 & 171-173).

family and the future of children and social work, it cannot be meaningful without this divorce that is so intimately bound to the 'new and strange definition of family' in Canada. I will therefore have to draw from the divorce proceedings and consequences from time to time. I will presently do so to concretize the confusion thesis with a bit more of what brought about the contradiction, a fact that also addresses the future of social work. I lost my job in 2006 because of the several court appearances (for child support, child custody, and divorce) I had to make in London, Ontario (which is eight hours drive from Montréal, Québec: meaning about three working days lost every court session). The given reason was "reorganization" since my company could not have openly stated that it was firing me for over-attending to court sessions. Things went from bad to worse on me that, after a long time searching (to no avail,) for just anything to do, I ended up on last resort assistance (social welfare). My ex-wife's interpretation to her friends (who were knowing only then from her that I had been paying child support) was simply that this was my ploy to make her suffer because the child support "was helping me a lot." Here then are two important questions for Social Work Canada in particular and for believers in professionals.

First, if a registered social worker does not know that social welfare is not accorded simply because you present yourself for it but because, after a keen study of your case, it is found that you deserve it, then who should know? My ex-wife in particular does not even need to be a social worker to have this knowledge because in 2001 Scholastica actually went requesting for social welfare behind my back and her application was rejected because she could not satisfy the requirements since she was then living with me and I was working and supporting her. Second, if the *child support* is actually to support the children, then will your not being able to pay it because you are on welfare make but *the children to suffer* or their mother? Yet, I am still paying the arrears of child support that accumulated during those years I was unable to find a job and on government assistance, largely because Scholastica and her parents do see child support not as a responsibility (that I have towards my children that are not

85

leaving with me) but as a source of enrichment and/or some sort of punishment for whatever crime they pin on me, including my being truthful about my children – with and without her. As you can then see, lies are never consistent; only the truth is consistent. Avoiding lying therefore, I had told my Yaoundé questioners that I had to go through some other person who was to take me to Michael's.

To the question regarding where this other person lives, I was again oblivious but had to go to his office to meet him. And where is that office? American Embassy was the response. What a nasty coincidence! The insistent guy was now more than triumphant while the other was convinced. The next thing I heard was their call for the policemen in uniform to *"amener ce gars au poste."* I was locked up without further ado for about two days and all the money I had worked so hard for, as well as that contributed by the friends in Garoua and Ngaoundéré, was seized (stolen) by these rogues in uniform. When I was finally released, all I got was *"Tu peux partir"* and when I asked about the money and other items they had taken from me, *"de quel argent parles-tu?"* was the question to my question.

I left the police *poste* of the Yaoundé train station very determined to get out of that city; although how, I was still to figure out. I had no money but money, I reassured myself, is not all that there is to success. That is cleanly a larger picture person's way of life. In my place there at the Yaoundé train station a narrow-minded and money-focused person would surely be so confused and perhaps desperately die because of the lack of money. I am clearly not like that; and I am sure I was even released from the train station cell solely because my story was found not to be inconsistent or bogus. I began finding my way to the American Embassy to meet the only contact I had in town. I inquired from one person how far the embassy was from there and he told me it was farther than I could imagine and that I needed to catch a cab to get there or take and connect about two or three city buses. The second said it was just around the corner and I therefore approached a third who happened to be English-speaking and had more patience in directing me how to get there, indicating with approximate traffic lights how far to go on a boulevard or street before meeting this or that other street and turning right or left etc. I quickly scribbled all this down and although it was quite a trek, his helpful guides shortened it considerably. I finally reached the Embassy of the United States of America about an hour and half before closing time. Mr. X (a Bangwa man whose names I have long forgotten) came down to see me and asked me to wait until closing time when he would take me to Michael's home. At last I was feeling like something good was happening in Yaoundé. When we got to Total Melen where Michael was then residing and, finding that he was not in town but elsewhere on holiday, Mr. X (who had been duly briefed of my train-station ordeal) abandoned me there, boarded a taxi and took off. What was I to do?

Luckily, I have learnt not to despair in such circumstances but to wisely ask questions. I stopped a passerby that I had staked from a distance and asked where the university was. He pointed over a hill from where we were standing and I demanded further how to get there and he said I should go through Château. In my later years in the UNIYAO I realized that it was about five to ten minutes walk passing through CUSS (the University Health Sciences Centre) that was on the other side of the road. Being new to town, I had to take the long way through Carrefour EMIA to Château and down to Ngoa-Ékéllé. It was September and there were students on campus to re-sit the subjects they had failed in during the June session. I was moving with ears wide open for anyone speaking English since, it seemed then, they were proving to be more helpful to me in this 'crazy' city. Without knowing, I was already around the student residential area when I heard some Njangawatok (Pidgin) in one of the stairs. I followed it until I knocked at the door and they opened it.

A bit relieved but extremely hungry and tired, I narrated what had happened to me on my arrival in town about three days before and asked if they had anything to eat. Much as they sympathized with me and, above all, glad that I was very fortunate to have been released and still alive, they unfortunately had no food. But, unknown to them, they instead offered me something that was far more

87

important than food – post-dated student train ticket to Douala! My hunger and fatigue suddenly varnished at the mention of the ticket even though they indicated that I could only use it in a few days time, not immediately. I asked for the ticket and how to get back to the train station that same evening and one of them, seeing how determined I was to get out of Yaoundé, also offered me a bus ticket, explaining in detail how and where to connect. His task was made a lot easier by the bus experience I had acquired in Douala while I had been desperately job-hunting there. I thanked them plentifully and said goodbye.

Without the bus ticket, I obviously would not have made it to the train station in time. The controllers in the train had signalled that the problems attached to my post-dated ticket would be looked into at the Douala train station. Recalling how these Francophones presume guilt before anything else, I wisely avoided those other Douala-train-station troubles by jumping out of the moving train when it was somewhere in New Bell, Douala – some distance before the final station in Bonanjo, Douala. At this point my mind had crystallized on leaving Cameroon for any English-speaking country, Nigeria being the natural choice since it was the only such bordering country, and I also did not then have money and travelling documents.

Nigeria via Bamenda and Back to Yoke

After a week or so in Douala, I left for Bamenda (the capital of North West Region) where I unknowingly entered into a tiger's mouth but my instincts got me out in time before it could gnaw; all thanks largely also to my belief that, as crucial as it is, money is not all that matters for one to succeed. Arriving Bamenda and having nowhere to stay while waging the "becoming better" war, I naturally navigated to Mile Two Nkwen where I had learnt one of papa's co-workers from the Yoke Powercam Camp was then residing. The homeowner first suggested that I go back to Yoke and control his sand business there, giving me the freedom to do whatever I wanted to with money from the business. I had not shown any interest in his proposal; my reasoning being that if that was such a great opportunity why was his own son, who had obtained the Advanced Level the same year as me, not running his business that he so liberally wanted but me to run? It was only after my return to Yoke from Nigeria that I learned that everyone that has been that connected to the man's sand business has had to die mysteriously. Finding the sand business thing not to be catching my attention, he began insisting that I go hunting with him in the night. I never obeyed my host's demands and left for my own place even as things were so hard on me, still believing strongly that money alone is not what is essential for success. This segment of my roaming days is dominated by the money idea, a handmaiden of which is that the gift may be little to the giver but may mean the world to the recipient.

Money Is Not All There Is to Success: The Interviews and the BIROCOL (and Other) Money Affairs

Two factors had particularly propelled my decision to perch at the home in Mile Two Nkwen. First, the madam of the house is such a nice, understanding, and selfless woman that I have often wondered why my mother was not like her. Second, their first son (who was by no means the eldest in the house) was in CCAS Kumba with me, being one class ahead of me though we had both obtained the G.C.E. Advanced Level the same year. He was a boarding student in CCAS doing the same A3 option as me. Because I could not afford going home for the *midi* break and then coming back for the afternoon session, I used to stay around his bed while they were taking siesta; often reading some of his books since I could not afford to buy all the books then. I saw this Bamenda stay as a perfect occasion to also thank him for his help, unwitting as it was.

But the guy's reaction simply told me that, had he been in the least aware of my G.C.E. bid, he would very well have hidden all his books from me. For example, he had secured a teaching position with Our Lady of Lourdes College, Mankon (Bamenda) after the G.C.E. results. At the time I was in Bamenda, he had passed the

89

Sonel (Société nationale de l'éléctricité) examination into the corporation's training school and I asked if he could recommend me for his Lourdes position but he flatly told me the place had already been filled. It was a plain lie as I later discovered on going there by myself. In Lourdes I was made to understand that he had abandoned the position and never responded to their repeated requests for him to bring along someone to replace him. They had thereafter contacted a former student of theirs (who had enrolled in the UNIYAO but was contemplating abandoning it) to see if she could come and fill the post. Nevertheless, they asked me to come back in two weeks by which time if the former student had not shown up they could offer me the position, the absent senior Sister also to be around by then to make the decision. I kept my fingers crossed and continued teaching economics and English language at the Progressive Institute of Stenography (PIS) around the Pharmacy Junction, having already been there for close to two weeks before the close of the month. I was hired there on a monthly salary of fourteen thousand (14,000) francs CFA and as soon as I received my dues for the first two weeks there, I got a place for myself around the Bamenda Hospital, despite that I so badly needed to save as much money for the Nigerian trip, a thing to be easily and quickly done by continuing to stay at Mile Two Nkwen.

But whenever my instincts (or the small but clear voices inside my head) come calling I scarcely hesitate in answering; this having proven to be a unique ingredient of success for me. It was precisely because of the swift answering to the call, for instance, that I also stumbled on a Muyuka acquaintance at the University of Calabar, Nigeria, at a time and place when/where just meeting someone I know was so critical to surviving. As a construction worker and spending the nights in the tools and materials compartment on a construction site in Calabar (imagine the high exposure to being killed there by thieves!), I had this strong feeling one evening that I should visit the city's university (that I was planning to enrol in after finding my feet in the place) to have an idea of what the milieu looks like. You can imagine what most people in my shoes here would do:

90

work every hour and day to make the money first and as fast as possible. Not this guy who almost always answers to his instincts.

The next morning as the others arrived for work, I approached the supervisor who immediately asked: "What now, Cameroon boy?" That is the way everyone was referring to me because my intonation is something I just cannot hide or change. From day one as soon as I opened my mouth to say anything, "Na Cameroon boy be this" was always the general observation. To date, a lot of people even doubt (my being from abroad) when I am in Cameroon and some relatives keep introducing me as their "brother from Canada" because of my unchanged Cameroonian inflection. Anyway, I had explained to my construction site supervisor that I needed the day off to take care of some pressing issues emanating from home, Cameroon. His hands were obviously full and it was so abrupt but the brusqueness coupled well with the fact that I was not known to be the off-day taking guy to make my case very compelling. He gave in and I took off, not even knowing exactly where I was going to; only being propped up by the reflection that if I had made it to Nigeria and down to Calabar with almost practically no money, what was there to keep me from finding my way in Calabar then when I even had some money?

I was just as marvelled at the University of Calabar campus (comparing with what I had seen in the UNIYAO in Cameroon) as I had been at the roads leading out of Takum, the first bordering village town (by Nigerian standards) but more than a city by Cameroonian scales. In fact, if I had not actually entered Nigeria trekking through the border but by air, I would have plainly disputed that I was still in the Africa I was (until then) used to, let alone in neighbouring Nigeria. The difference was simply staggering. What could be responsible for such gapping differences between two neighbouring African states? Could it be attributable to the disparate colonial legacies; to the federal nature of Nigeria; or to what else?[10]As I was swaggering around that campus, lost in thoughts and totally

---

[10] For some possible and convincing answers to the query, see Fossungu (2013b); and Fossungu (2013a: chapter 5).

oblivious of the suffering at the construction site (the only Calabar I had known till then), I was startled by a voice calling out "Figaro!" Who could be calling 'Na Cameroon Boy be this' in Nigeria by that name? I thought I was actually dreaming, not just day-dreaming and had to slap myself hard in order to wake up. There he was, smiling and saying "It is not a dream, it is not Muyuka, it is me, Vahid, and we are both in Calabar, Nigeria now. What are you doing here?" The feeling was just awe-inspiring. I recognized Vahid Ashu as the Muyuka boy living not far from the Catholic Mission church and school in Strangers Quarter but I did not know his name until then. Did I have a short and precise answer to Vahid's question like I did to the Lourdes Sister's?

I had excitedly gone back for the Lourdes rendezvous after the two-week period. The lady they had been waiting upon had still not come and I had a small chat (or should I say interview?) with the Sisters. I am not the type that would camouflage who I really am just to obtain someone's favours, let alone what I know I merit acquiring. Staying true to self has been another indispensable ingredient of success and failure of mine, both in and outside the household. I think I got that also from my father's training because papa was very organized, disciplined and disciplinary; wanting all his children to learn to be responsible both individually and collectively. Thus, when his return from work approached, no one was at ease at home. Just don't be the first person he encounters at the scene if, say, a pan is not in the right place. Just get the pan to where it is supposed to be and never say 'I don't know' to his question 'Who put this pan here?' If you do, he will counter: "Good Gracious! You don't know, so who should know? Or, if it is a spirit that put it there, did you not see it, and why is it still there?" Some people who do not like strict people would jump to describe papa as 'wicked' because his love for following rules and for hardworking folks was hardly turned over.

In the course of the Lourdes interview, one of the Sisters (as I suspected, the senior one) asked what I must have been thinking appearing for the appointment the way I had. I was not going to pretend that I did not get her point to be asking for further

92

enlightenment as she had expected. She wanted me, in brief, to come in a way that would give the impression that I was someone that would not be interested at all in dating some of the female students I was going to be teaching. Much as I was then not even interested in any other woman, and much as you know I needed that job, I merely pointedly asked back: "With all due respect, Sisters, which is more dangerous dealing with – a wolf that openly comes to you as a wolf or one appearing in sheep skin?" With this question-response, I heard the former student tale all over again and knew right there that their promise to get back to me was mere hypocrisy passing for politeness; just as the then principal of Bopson Comprehensive College in Nkwen, Bamenda, who (from my understanding of his funny behaviour) actually wanted me to come and "see him with oil for his mouth" before I could fill the vacant position in his college. This Bangwa man who, by some later strange happenings, has one of the aunties of my ex-wife as wife just did not know the calibre of the man he was dealing with. Imagine (from Chapter 4 below) the great things that some of the students in both Lourdes and Bopson actually missed from me just because of a handful of twisted-minded individuals.

But those twisted-minded people were not the only that made my Bamenda passage both difficult and memorable. It was in Bamenda that I also reunited with my only full-blood sibling, Dieudonné, after about sixteen years of growing apart. Dieudonné had just completed primary school and (because there was no one to send him to college) was in Bamenda, living with a maternal relation and learning tailoring and bricklaying, successively. It was supposed to be a real splendid moment and time to catch up on the lost years but it did not turn out to be so because of the 'becoming better' pressure I was under. By this time I had moved back to Nkwen where I was putting up with Uncle Gabriel Nkwetta Fossungu who I had met during the many visits to Bopson Comprehensive College where he was then studying together with many other Fossungu cousins.

I had a lot of dresses, no doubt, and it had even become one of the household's complaint sing-songs that I had "things even more

93

than a working class." But at that time I was not going around with a lot of dresses and shoes but a lot more of my certificates and other documents. Dieudonné is a lot taller than me but we wear the same shoe size. So, apart from a few bigger and longer shirts, I let him have almost all the pairs of shoes but one that I needed to be using especially when I needed to attend an interview that required suiting up. One day while I was behind taking my bath in preparation for an interview with Nacho Comprehensive College there in Bamenda, Dieudonné came in and, against Uncle Nkwetta's counsel, took away that last pair of shoes, saying "Why is he my brother if I cannot take the pair of shoes?" I do not know whether this was destined but I missed the appointment, not being the only candidate for it as was the case in Lourdes. I was so crossed that when my brother later showed up and was behaving as if it was nothing, for the first time I raised my hand and hit him before I could hold back myself. It is one of those few very devastating things I have had to regret ever doing because it kind of instilled the fear of me and a permanent freeze in Dieudonné that has been kind of difficult to take away, especially as we scarcely had any time together thereafter because I left for Nigeria.

The main things on my mind in Nkambe (as I was waiting to have some Nigeria-bound cross-border traders with whom to make *The Long Trek* and even during the entire trek) were the Bishop Rogan College (BIROCOL) money affair and this issue of people always nosing around for information about things that do not even concern them. That is why only Uncle Nkwetta knew that, and when, I was to leave Bamenda for Nigeria. These issues dominated my trek out of Cameroon since I was trying to see if my not partaking in the habit could have been costly to my bid for university education. I have this nag for saying things without having any evidence at the time of speaking, with them then turning out to be as if I had the evidence before opening my mouth. Some would call it intuition, and which most of the time (in my case) is tied to ignorance; the type of lack of knowledge that results from the fact that you are not accustomed to nosing around for information like some journalists accuse some

94

Cameroonian lawyers of doing (see Fossungu, 2013b: 147);or what Ivoirians popularly refer to as looking for history where there is no geography (*"chercher l'histoire là où il n'y a pas la géographie"*). For example, what would you say is actually behind a divorce case (except the desire to extract so-called child support) when the petitioner gets her demands but would continue year after year policing, by nosing around for information in regard of, the respondent and his relationships?

Nosing around for information or being a "curious Johnny" is not always bad. For example, papa always opened my letters that came care of him. He is not supposed to do that. But on two out of three occasions it was very helpful that he did so; otherwise, I would have missed the critical employment opportunity in Collège de l'Unité de Manjo that is discussed below in chapter 4. He speedily came up with the letter to Yoke the same day and I left for Manjo (in the Littoral Region), reaching there just in time before the lapse of the offer. Again, I would not have had my acceptance slip for the G.C.E. Advanced Level in time since he was not even aware that I had registered for it. Opening and seeing what it was, he rushed with it to Kumba and I consequently got the necessary requirements and headed for Buea where I wrote the exam. I warmheartedly remember how, in dissuading me from (and warning about the dire consequences of) taking this G.C.E. Advanced Level in the lower sixth form, papa had wondered why "children nowadays are wont to want to fly to Jericho without having first developed and tested their own proper wings." When papa opened the letter a Manjo girlfriend wrote to me, it was in French and he could not read French although her enclosed photo was telling enough to make papa's knowledge of French irrelevant. He consequently only brought it up to Yoke during the weekend. "Curious-Johnnying" is therefore not always bad. I even consider it a kind of flaw in me that I do not sometimes do it, a clear instance being in regard of my half-siblings, especially Awandem who even came and lived with us in Yoke and I could not still divine his actual relationship to me. But for me, not nosing around has been more on the ingredient of success side than on that of a defect.

Always nosing around for information, for one thing, can easily instil in you what I call the Loser-Syndrome. That is one of the reasons I dislike it; and also tend to consider anyone who does it to be a loser. Of course, I cannot talk about my dislike for nosing around for information without talking about a Bamileke lady in Montreal I met after the London divorce. I had to call off the relationship with her especially because of this trait in her. Imagine sitting in a gathering with her and being asked whenever someone walks in or out: "Who is she? What does she do? How long has she been here in Montréal?" At the beginning I asked back: "How am I supposed to know all that, Gina?" believing she would realize that I am not interested in that attitude; but it only went from bad to worse; although not more frightening and deadly than dealing with unknown backstabbers as championed by the Bishop Rogan College (BIROCOL) and other money affairs that do also bring home necessary helpful information (that would have been wanting from my not nosing around for it) for better treading with the backstabbers.

My brother Bernard is squarely at the centre of the BIROCOL money affair that kept forcing its way into my head during the long trek into Nigeria. Joseph was boisterous, very disrespectful, and haughty but you would prefer dealing with him because you can easily predict his moves, unlike introverts of the household like Bernard (*Coastman*). By some curious ways of nature, the introverts were separated by the non-introverts in their birth positions. You will hardly know what is in store for you from such people until it has actually happened; making them even more dangerous. Take a very serious case of Bernard's duplicity, namely, the attempt on papa's life at his *njumba*'s home in Yoke. When this happened, Joseph's name was written all over it, with Bernard having thereafter taken off to Wum in the North West Region for holidays at his namesake's. Fon ST Fossungu (our grandpa) had to come down to Yoke to find out what could have propelled a child to such an abominable act. On being questioned by His Royal Highness, Joseph declared that he had nothing whatsoever to say to anybody whosoever until his partner,

96

Coastman, was also brought in. It was only then that anyone outside the duo (or trio?) shockingly knew Bernard had been part and parcel of the entire plot against both papa and his *njumba,* Madam Catherine. Perhaps *Coastman*'s middle name, Mbancho (*battlefield* or *battleground* in Bangwa), was very apt?

Again, Bernard was in BIROCOL in Small Soppo, a stone throw from Sasse College where I was. I once had some real and pressing financial difficulties at school and wrote to papa for help. Since my mother had become a regular visitor to BIROCOL when Ben got there, papa (in response to my need and request) sent some money to me through her. She never came to Sasse College but left the amount with Ben who I saw often when we had outings. No mention of the money was ever made. During the following holiday, papa never heard me thanking him, as usual, for the money sent to me, so he asked what the matter was. Thanks to papa for being the type that speaks out his mind, the smear campaign failed.

I am fond of people like papa who speak out their mind when they realize something is not going well. As I always tell people around me, remember always that those who never disagree with you are either your stooges or enemies. These are those that gossip about you since they do not have the courage to tell you what they think about you (or your stance on issues) in your face. That he who listens to gossip and does nothing to stop this gossiping, himself gossips. If I tell you, for instance, that I saw Yoyo stealing something, the best thing to do is to have Yoyo and I present and then ask me to repeat what I had told you about Yoyo. If I cannot then say it again, then it is gossiping that it was and you would have also stopped it because I would not have the guts to come to you again with any more gossips. There are therefore two simple reasons why I particularly like when someone corrects or criticizes my errors. First, I know I am human and, second, I know I am dealing with another human, not a monster that would devour me when I am not looking. That is why if I were Cameroon's president, I would fire all 'collaborators' that never disagree with me; including those that do so only to eschew being fired for not disagreeing, for these are even more dangerous.

97

Unlike my father in the BIROCOL money case under discussion, my father-in-law, Peter Ngunyi Asahchop, cannot speak out his mind and thus helps in disseminating gossip or blackmail, if not actually initiating and promoting it. In October 2002 I lost my father. Friends in Montréal, Gatineau, and Edmonton donated whatever they could to assist me in my trip to Cameroon for the burial. But my wife instead lent me a thousand dollars which I duly repaid after my return from Cameroon because, being who I am, I see a loan as a loan, not a gift (notwithstanding that she was lending me money while still wholly 'parasiting' on me, to use her own words). Before I had reached Cameroon for my dad's burial, however, Scholastica had communicated with her father, telling him she had sent a thousand dollars (1000.00$) to him through me. I arrived and after the ceremony in Nwangong I visited my parents-in-law in Fontem and spent two or three nights there. All along the house was always full of visitors (their friends and neighbours) that, of course, I needed to entertain; and all along my father-in-law kept saying "we haven't talked". All the time I would be waiting for him to introduce the talk to no avail. I never actually understood him until I left and eventually returned to Canada. As already indicated, I repaid the loan to his daughter, my wife.

It was not until June 2004 when I again visited Cameroon (after my father-in-law had died in February that year) that I understood he had been very angry with me, having written to Fon DF Fossungu (the Fon was kind enough to let me have that letter) and bitterly complaining about my disrespect for him and his entire family. (Is it not amazing that someone who disrespects you is right there with you and you cannot tell him that to his face, but wait till he is gone and you talk about it to others?) Knowing me the Fon did not believe it to be true. He had then inquired to know just how I could have been that callous towards my in-laws and my father-in-law then narrated to him the entire story of his daughter sending him money through me and that I never handed it over. What a way to give a dog a bad name! How many more of such contrivances are out there around my name and person? Why did Scholastica's father not squarely confront me by directly and cleanly asking for the money that had supposedly been sent to him through me, like papa did concerning the money he had sent to me but got no thank you in return? Wouldn't that have been what to expect from a bold and truthful father-in-law especially?

Take also my mother-in-law's case since we are now not only talking money affairs and their roles in the definition of family and children's future but also talking about unknown backstabbers. I do not usually do anything because I want to go about boasting about it. But, as Chinua Achebe has again said, the lizard that successfully jumped from the high iroko tree said it would congratulate itself if no one else did. The parental role is very important in the shaping of the future of children; being intimately tied to the truthfulness of parents and other relations. That is why I will here talk a bit about Scholastica's mother's backstabbing attitude that augurs badly not only to the definition of family but also to children's future, using her callous ingratitude generally, and particularly in regard of the five hundred thousand francs CFA that I sent to her through Western Union in February 2004 when she lost her husband. I sent this money to her directly because it was meant to assist in the decent burial of her husband (my father-in-law), knowing full well what assisting her through third parties (like members of my extended family) would entail. I had tried to get to her directly to pass on the information on the funds transfer but for some reasons (of nature) her phone was not going through despite all the numerous attempts. That is when I thought of getting the information to her through Violet Malatey Fossungu (now Fonenge), a cousin who was then studying linguistics in the University of Dschang. Nature alone knows why Scholastica's mother's phone never went through; otherwise, no one would be aware that I had assisted at all in the ceremony since my mother-in-law hid the money; not even informing the rest of the members of the dead man's family of it; and all this even as everyone was condemning the fact that I (as the most pronounced in-law to the deceased) was playing no role in the matter. It was only Violet (a cousin also to Scholastica!) who later brought

99

home the news of the sum that I had sent to my mother-in-law for the purpose when the libel had already gotten out of hand.

Is that the way a bold and truthful mother-in-law (desirous of the wellbeing of her children and grandchildren) should comport herself? It obviously looks like there is a complete 'family' plot to disparage me in view, perhaps, of whitewashing gross thanklessness and devilish scheme. Otherwise, why couldn't my parents-in-law have acted like papa? When I had told papa I never received any money, the BIROCOL money smear campaign failed because papa immediately called his wife who said she had left it with Bernard and Bernard then went into his box, got the money and returned it to papa. The money therefore never reached me nor solved my problem but the important thing at that point was the fact that papa knew that I was not the ungrateful kid that his not being bold and truthful would have created of me in his mind.

The other important question is: Was Bernard acting on his mother's instruction or merely preventing me, in his own way, from "eating our father's money"? I am not the vengeful type but Bernard paid in a way for his monkey business, including always making me prepare many dishes at home for no good reason. *Coastman* is the type that claims he does not eat this or that simply because I would be asked to prepare a different dish that his whims and caprices would choose. One of his favourite 'don't-eats' is *ndolé* (bitter herbs). One day we came back from the farm and mother who had stayed behind had not yet cooked anything. We were tired of "drinking garri" on such occurrences; so Bernard and I headed to one of those Yoke houses where for sure we would be served some food, precisely at Sam's Mother's. It was delicious *ndolé* and boiled ripe plantains that Sam's Mother put before us. After about two spoonfuls, I asked Bernard if he had started eating *ndolé*. He then pretended not to have known and asked if it was *ndolé* and outspoken Sam's Mother quickly and happily confirmed. He stopped eating and did not vomit or have any problem as would normally be the case for someone that has eaten what s/he was allergic to. I thus "wiped" the food alone, my intention not having been to deny him satisfaction of his hunger but

100

to have him come clean of his pretence. He chose not to do so and therefore bore the consequence of his dishonesty.

As Sam's Mother had explained afterwards to me, very happy that I had asked the *ndolé*-eating question just at the right moment, "I think I understand Ben's problem well enough. He is a heavy eater and people like him need much time to do it slowly and surely; a thing that he does not get eating from the same bowl with the rest of you. Therefore, he has to find a way of having a dish all to himself but rather than say so plainly, he prefers the dubious manner." This duplicity, I was bound to conclude, had a big hand in my then arriving in a strange country like Nigeria without money and after spending many nights in an unknown forest. We spent about three to five nights in the forest and when we arrived in Takum I was sort of relieved but very worried since (being new in the affair) the uniform boys on both sides had taken so much of the money I had that what I still had left in Takum was purely insufficient to get me to Calabar. A huge lesson on gifts was learnt in Takum and beyond.

The Philosophy of Gifts: Defying African and Canadian Definitions of Family

I got the nicknames *Professor* and *Lord Denning* while I was studying in the UNIYAO (to leave out *Read this Classic Paper* in CCAS Kumba) because of the way I usually extensively "poured stuff" in support of my points; and I am not about to do otherwise here with the analysis of the new definition of family that is wholly out of place, whether viewed from the African context or the Canadian. This strangely new definition of family is in reality just the tip of the iceberg of the parental spell and scheming to the total disregard of children's future that I am talking about as well as condemning. For Scholastica, this spell was there even at the marriage-decision stage (as seen in chapter 5) but was aggravated and entrenched especially during the four years I was away studying in Montréal, Canada (1995-99); in the course of which Scholastica must have fallen completely under the hex of her scheming parents. So was it an error for me to

101

have left lectureship at the University of Buea in Cameroon in 1995 for further studies in McGill University? I pose some of these questions because, just like the lay persons deserve to know from the intellectuals,[11] I think a child also rightly deserves to know if, when and why his or her parents' marriage is not working as others he or she finds around him or her; and that parents that conspire not tell this child the truth (at some point) do not deserve to be parents to that child in the first place. The truth regarding the failure of the Peter-Scholastica family/marriage therefore impels my discussing the new definition of family in the context of the giver-receiver philosophy.

Some of the essential lessons I acquired in Takum are that the Giver's Little Gift Can Mean the World to the Recipient; and that those who can never give cannot quite appreciate whatever someone else gives to them. Put differently, the take-and-take-and-take people, never having been on the giving side, can hardly be appreciative of what they just keep receiving. The 'Four-Eyes' Mathematical Equation in this scenario becomes "Give and Take versus Take and Take and Take". If I again apply my knowledge of arithmetic here, as I did while still in primary school to coin the *Big Mami Trouble* concept seen in Chapter 1, then one of the three 'takes' on the right cancels the only other on the other side, leaving one side to continue indefinitely giving while the other continues endlessly taking and taking; with an obvious accentuated destabilizing imbalance that does necessarily un-define the other side; and thus also un-defining (and 'redefining') family. That, in a nutshell, describes the nature of the relationship between Scholastica and Peter. Two or three gifts (including one that changed from a loan) will make the point, namely,

---

[11]"I think the lay persons deserve to know from the intellectuals why their country is not working as others they find around them; and that intellectuals that cannot tell them the truth do not deserve to be intellectuals to begin with because I am made to know that the role of the intellectual (whatever the sex of this Janus) is to shed light (and not to engender darkness) on the issues, controversial as they may be" (Fossungu, 2013a: at viii-ix, note omitted).

(1) the Takum gift (and the Loan and Plane Ticket) from God and (2) the Nwangong generator gift of June 2004.

The Takum Gift (and the Loan and Plane Ticket) from God

Calculating in Takum with the traders who were heading to Abba and Onitsha, the money I had left could take me only as far as Katsina Alla. Do I know anyone there, they inquired. Good thing I still kept in touch with my Yoke and Sasse College pal, Celestine Anusiem, who was then in the University of Nsukka. I told them the only person I knew in the country was in Nsukka and there was some amount of relief on their part. Remember that I only became these traders' acquaintance at the point in Nkambe (Cameroon) where the trekking started but they were here contributing some naira to permit me reach Nsukka in the hope of meeting Celestine Anusiem who was not at all aware I was coming. What if you cannot find your friend in Nsukka, one of the traders asked. Very grateful for their kind and brotherly gesture, I merely responded:

When destiny calls, I have to answer present. I did not anticipate this particular money problem; maybe if I did I would not be here right now. But the issue has surfaced stiffly and just see what you guys have done; may God bless you all very bountifully. I would therefore not want to worry about what problems Nsukka has in store until I am in Nsukka. Once more, I am indescribably grateful for your kind-heartedness.

This advice then becomes important. Always know that before becoming an expert, the expert was a no-expert and would obviously have remained a no-expert if he or she never did what transformed him or her into an expert until he or she was already an expert. I fondly remember telling Scholastica in Douala in 1994 that we were going to go to Canada and her quick question was "Where would the money come from?" My answer to her quiz was that there are a lot of other things to succeeding in life than just having the money on hand. As a larger picture person, and growing up with papa, I have come to see money not solely in terms of the amount of it staked up in a bank account but mostly in terms of what money can do to alleviate some of the sufferings I find all around me.

When I say papa was very rich, for instance, I am not just referring to what he had as money (and he had lots of it too). I also look at his capacity to put money to the service of people. In my bid to attend McGill University in 1995 papa gave me the required amount for the bank statement and I was counting on selling my car to obtain the flight ticket. But that did not work even at the last minute because prospective buyers were offering amounts not near the value of the car or the amount for the air ticket (CFA 800,000francs). The arrival deadline given to me by McGill University was fast drawing near and I had already tried other alternatives to no avail. As a last resort, Scholastica and I drove from Douala to Yoke to see papa who was then retired.

In view of what papa had already done that far, I was not surprised by his indication that there was nothing left in his account. But Madam Catherine (then his legal wife) interceded, pleading with him to help me in whatever way to surmount this last obstacle. Papa said okay and went into his bedroom. He was in there for quite some time and my thinking was that he was getting ready for us to drive down to Victoria or to another bank, perhaps in Muyuka. To my surprise, when he came out, he gave a packet of eight hundred thousand francs CFA to his wife to give to my wife and I to count and be sure that he did not make an error. It was Scholastica that did the counting and confirmed. I would not want to go into describing the emotion but instead just highlight two things that go straight into the basket of the ingredients of success, with or without money. The first is that I was able to overcome this particular obstacle because I had not taken sides in the quarrel between Mami Thecla, on one side, and Madam Catherine, on the other; and, second, my not being bitter after being dropped by papa in 1981 (the roaming days which I am now discussing) – some fourteen years before. All of these could not have been possible if I were not the kind that would always look at the larger picture of things, knowing full well that money alone is not all that is important to succeeding in life.

Four years after the Yoke Flight-Ticket Money Incident, Scholastica herself was joining me in Montréal, Canada in April 1999. Where did the money for her schooling and upkeep in Buea during those four years, and for her trip and stay here in Canada till 2004 (when she began working) come from? And was it just the money that really counted? Now, if I say I have a problem with people like Scholastica who cross the river and burn the bridge to prevent other persons from also crossing, a lot of narrow-minded people would restrict 'other persons' here to my own brothers, sisters, and parents. This is not exactly correct to a larger picture person. I well remember Nancy Whistance-Smith (of Edmonton, Alberta) narrating some very negative experiences they had had in Kenya (Africa) and how, because of those, they had vowed never to trust Africans. But that negativity toward Africans, she had concluded, completely changed when they met and interacted with me. That is precisely the reason they had been lending us (Scholastica and I) as much as they have had to in order to enable us do all what we have done.

I particularly have no problem with Scholastica's ingratitude toward my person, but I would be lying if I say do not have one when she extends this to those (like my father and Andrew and Nancy Whistance-Smith) who have so sumptuously helped me to help her and her family (which she has, since arriving Canada and becoming a Canadian permanent resident, defined as composing of only herself, brothers, sisters, parents). You would better grasp the point if you imagine the great friends I once had in Edmonton (Alberta, Canada) who believed so much in Peter and Scholastica (without even having met her in person). Scholastica and I both know very well that we were supposed to have paid back close to twenty-one thousand dollars (interest-free) that the Whistance-Smiths lent us. This sum includes the one thousand five hundred dollars (1500.00$) they sent to us in 2000 when Scholastica's permanent residence application deadline was proving difficult to meet. But that is not all. But for their generous loan of seven hundred dollars every month, plus letter of undertaking, I would never have gotten my student authorization for, and completed, the doctoral programme at

Université de Montréal in Canada; and Scholastica would also never have done same in the University of Buea in Cameroon, let alone join me in Canada in 1999. More than twelve years now since I graduated from Montréal, more than thirteen since Scholastica arrived in Canada, more than eight since she began working professionally, we have not yet paid a dime to people who made all these things happened. Yet, Scholastica can afford to own a home in Canada and vacation in Hawaii, Florida, Niagara, etc, while I (who no longer feature as anything in her definition of family) also pay four hundred and twenty-eight dollars (428.00$) every month to her (as support for children that are also not part of her definition of family) rather than to our creditors. If Scholastica considers this fair game, I clearly don't. I wonder whether she has also refused to repay her student loan to the Canadian Government.

But it is not just about the money that I am talking here; most of you would just not want to believe that the Whistance-Smiths have already written off the debt! I am talking more about (1) honouring one's engagement with others and (2) the future of children and social work. Respecting engagements makes life much more meaningful to the many people behind you since you do not burn the bridge after you have crossed it. Come to imagine the number of other (African) persons who, had we already repaid or were repaying their loan, would already have also benefitted from the kind heartedness of this wonderful Canadian family, including those lining up behind them (like Scholastica and her brothers, sisters and parents have been behind me): then you will get the bigger picture I am talking about. Also come to think about the future of 'our' children growing up in a two-parent home of a registered social worker as mother and a university law professor (or practising lawyer) as father and you will adequately grasp the larger picture I am alluding to.

The larger picture I am talking about here is a thing that can hardly be grasped by someone who sees only take and take and take as the rule in life; a perspective that obviously does not portend well with the future of children that, moreover, are not part of the outlandish definition of family – *absolument sans enfants et mari*! That

106

being case, here then is one essential puzzle for believers in professionals and for Social Work Canada in particular: If a person's definition of family is 'I, my brothers, my sisters, and my parents', I visibly think that person noticeably cannot be counselling people whose definition of family is 'my spouse, our children, and me'. I wonder then whether such a person can be able to correctly divine what would be important in the case of those having a different definition of family. What therefore is the future of your children (who are not in her definition of family) if there are some nascent problems in your family and a social worker of this calibre is assigned to your case? What hope for social work with such social workers?

Whatever the case with their future, as I have already mentioned, only givers do truly appreciate gifts as receivers; which could elucidate why those appreciative words of mine to the traders in Takum, coming from the bottom of my heart and watered by the tears of joy that were flowing while they were being uttered, were so touching to one of the traders that he offered me an additional three hundred naira saying: "Take this, my son; you will surely be needing it. I have never seen anyone with your courage and determination. May the lord bless and guide you." It was as if he had just opened the floodgates because the further individual donations from most of them truthfully weighed me down. The feeling I had at that moment could only be compared to the one in Nwangong in June 2004, in another unplanned gift situation that caused me to break one of my golden rules of not making promises beforehand.

The Nwangong Generator Gift in June 2004

In June 2004 I made a short-notice trip to Cameroon to attend to my sick and frail birth mother in the village, at the time living with a younger relation of hers in Nwancheng quarter. I had a small surprise gift for the people of Nwangong; a village which, like so many others in Cameroon, does not have electricity. Reaching the village, I got the keys to papa's house in Letia quarter from the palace. Papa's house is where I usually stay (to date) when in the village since my own building (on the other side of the road and not far from papa's) is yet

107

to be completed and ready for habitation. Papa had allocated part of his house in the village to be used as the village dispensary or health post. Many thoughts crossed my mind as I was setting things up in the visitor room: maybe I should concentrate more on the health post than the generator for the palace? There were many more questions on roads and the promotion of youth education and other training; but in the end I told myself to just do what I had in mind during this unplanned trip and look at the others later.

After I had bathed and eaten the next morning, I told the people who had then filled the house to welcome me that I had to go to Dschang, the closest town to Nwangong. When the cab got to Letia in the afternoon and the generator, other accessories (like connecting wires, bulbs and holders, more than enough for all the palace homes and those in its vicinity), television set and DVD player were being offloaded, the feast had commenced, the news of it spreading like dry season fire. Only four-wheel drives go down to the palace; but by the time the numerous spontaneous volunteers transporting the numerous boxes got there, there was already so much singing and dancing that triply augmented at the sight of the boxes. Unannounced as it was, food almost immediately started pouring in from both the Fon's wives and beyond. The non-Bangwa village nurse was surprised and happy as everyone else but still managed to very competently immortalize the occasion with the aid of a video camera.

Like papa in Kumba in 1972, Fon DF Fossungu was also obviously looking at the bigger picture in his 'Thank You' speech that evening of 22 June 2004. The Fon stated, first, that a good deed never walks alone, and he was sure it was just the start as my example was surely going to be imitated. In short, he was describing the gesture as a pioneering one that he was hoping would provoke similar undertakings from others. Second, the Fon told the people of Nwangong that "other people would only be entitled to minimize you if you do minimize yourself." The Fon noted, in the third place, that when Forbehndia (papa) was still up and doing, there was no end of year that people in the village did not "receive messages" from him; but that it was not a problem even then that papa was no longer alive, and rhetorically asking: "Is what we are having here this evening not still a message we are receiving from Forbehndia who trained and sent Dr. Nkemtale'eh to where he is coming from?" The others agreed that it was. "Some years back," the Fon carried on, "who would have believed that today we would also be sitting in this palace not with bush lamps but with bright shining electric bulbs hanging all over us?" No one at all, was the sonorous response. It seems that in the village speaking through rhetorical questions is a much cherished manner of involving listeners who consequently follow what you are saying better.

Saying a lot of good things, including the fact that all the receipts, duly handed over to him, were bearing the Fon's names and not the giver's, Fon DF Fossungu then stated that all this could only be indicative of the giver's wisdom and farsightedness for "with Dr. Nkemtale'eh back in Canada, could we be able to prove, in case we were going to repair any of these items and the police stopped us, that we did not steal them?" How could we, was the general response. As you can see, looking at the bigger picture of things becomes part and parcel of you when you have objectives such as those I have defined myself with. The Fon had then asked that I should come and stand at a position indicated and I think I heard the village nurse immediately saying "Wow! Dr. Fossungu is going to be awarded a medal!" That is exactly what happened and I asked her later how she knew and she explained: "I have lived in your village for quite long [eight months then] and have realized that your customs are not different in a lot of respects from those of Bafut. The Fon of Bafut does not tell someone about whom he is talking to come and stand here or there unless he wants to confer a medal on that person. And that is not something you see done often. Dr. Fossungu, people like you are rare to come by and I count myself very lucky to be your friend." I had to thank her for both the compliment and teaching on the medal awarding culture.

Personally placing the medal through my head onto my neck and lengthily justifying my meriting it, the Fon tersely added: "What I like so much about Dr. Nkemtale'eh is especially the fact that he never makes promises before doing anything. He just does it when he is ready to do it; which is very good because you can make promises and then find out after that you cannot keep them and thus become a liar." In a similar occasion in Canada, the then Cameroon Goodwill Association of Montreal (CGAM) President conferred the first "President Award on Dr. Peter Fossungu In recognition of your devotion and dedication to the cause of the Goodwill Association and for outstanding service rendered to the Association." Noting the recipient's versatility of character which is both complex and simple at the same time, the CGAM president particularly mentioned how, after handing over the CGAM presidency in January 2005, Dr. Fossungu continued serving in other capacities such as cameraman; combining this with Chief Whip in Ayah's second term in 2006. If CGAM President Ayah in December 2005 put it in terms that would require a lot of brains to grasp, another CGAM President, coming one president after Ayah, simplified the matter in August 2008 when "Dr. Peter Fossungu Is conferred the title of President Emeritus In recognition and appreciation of his exemplary leadership as pioneer president of GOODWILL."As CGAM President Folefac also noted on the occasion, "What I find particularly unique to Dr. Fossungu is his ability to so comfortably deal with or relate to people of diverse and differing educational levels and backgrounds, not to leave out their ethnic and cultural surroundings." Let us get back to Nwangong and the generator gift.

Many other speakers had also taken the floor (after the Fon of Nwangong) and attested to their gratitude and hopefulness in greater things to come into their lives. The general happiness that was pouring around for and from this little surprise gift of mine was so overwhelming to me that, in my response to the Fon's and other speeches on the occasion, I paradoxically broke the golden rule by making promises, especially to the youths of the village. I told them to take their studies very seriously because it is what has permitted me to be where I was coming from, promising those who did so some financial and other assistance up the minimum of high school, beginning the following academic year (2005/2006).

My promise to the youths of Nwangong has never happened and I have thus become a liar because of the type of woman I ended up with as wife. The spouse domain is a particular field in which I have always wanted to be better than my father, since it is an area which has been the stronghold of the forces working against and slowing down the advancement in his larger picture outlook on life. Paradoxically, it seems instead to be the one area in which I have had so many failures and un-defining moments that have, without a doubt, curtailed considerably the number of persons that would by now have made their way into "the greatest number of persons possible" whose lives I would already have ameliorated in ways far greater than the traders in Takum could ever have imagined when they were aiding me to at least reach Nsukka.

I spent three nights in the hostel of the University of Nsukka with Celestine Anusiem who was simply out of words when he met me. It was really a good break and rest from the long and dangerous trek through the forest. My friend suggested I hang around Nsukka but Calabar was the place I wanted to stick it out in, with my eyes set on UNICAL (University of Calabar). Anusiem did not only boost me up with financial help but also with a lot of reminiscences. "How is your sister Josephine, is she still acting as strange as I used to know her to?" Anusiem was always right about his observations in Josephine's regard because he just could not believe the excitement in his two senior sisters in Cameroon Baptist Academy when we often arrived there from Sasse College; whereas it was the contrary with my sister. He used to complain about something being wrong with Josephine and I often said there was not anything wrong with her that I knew of. This time in Nsukka I knew what the problem must have been but was not going to let the Josephine thing start marring my thoughts so I answered only the first part of Anusiem's query, indicating that Josephine was happily married with about three children then; and quickly turning the conversation to Sasse College and Yoke or Muyuka generally.

111

Muyuka has also been so vital in my struggles to advance not only because of the concentration there of the negative forces impacting on the definition of family and children in the household but also due to the fact that most of the positive movers that have unexpectedly popped up when I have been in some sort of dire strait have been tied to the town. Vahid from Muyuka, for example, had long finished his studies at the UNICAL and had come back there just to get some documents required for his Youth Service that he had been assigned to effect in Benin Kirbi in Sokoto State (as it then was). Vahid did not only give me all the information on how to join him there but also arranged with some acquaintances of his who were still in UNICAL for me to be spending the nights with them in the hostel until I was ready to make the trip up north. Sleeping on the floor in a university hostel was far safer and more eye-opening than at the construction site where I still worked during the day until I left for Benin Kirbi.

In this moderate northern city, I got to really know the calibre of the man called Vahid Ashu. I just cannot describe him enough but would merely advise that you must not go about leaving negative trails wherever you pass. If I did so, Vahid would never even have behaved that day at the UNICAL campus as if he knew me. That is exactly what he told me. In this connection, I also recall this young man stopping his car at a bus stop in Montréal where I had recently arrived and was waiting for the bus. Smiling very broadly at me, the young man's face was very familiar but I could not pin down exactly where I had known him when he refreshed my mind that I taught him at the UNIYAO and requested that I get into the car so that they (he was with his wife) could drop me off wherever I was going. Would this former student have even bothered stopping if I had been an obnoxious lecturer? You cannot be that when you are a person who always looks at the larger picture of things. I have even had to teach former Kumba primary school classmates in secondary school who later on were again my classmates in university. As Vahid (who was only then knowing my real name) had explained to me in Benin Kirbi, although we never really got the chance to know each other well enough in Muyuka, he always admired the fact that, flying as high as I then was, I was never boastful and mean as most others in my position would easily be. Do I still need to specifically identify that as an ingredient of success?

Vahid indeed worked as tirelessly as he could to secure me a teaching position in a secondary school in town; and it was nearing fruition when the Shehu Shagari re-election strategy of doing away with 'illegal' immigrants came in between. Vahid particularly talked me into staying and sticking it out but, knowing myself and what I was up against, I persisted and followed my instincts that were pointing straight to a return to Cameroon before things could get out of hand. Vahid at a point wondered if it was "that your black beauty" that was pulling me back to Yoke. Of course, a lady's invisible hand could not be completely put out of the equation but it was not the main reason for the U-turn. To begin with, there was just no way that I could have successfully passed for a Nigerian (from whatever part of it) like my friend. Second, I understood my new environment (experience also derived from staying in Garoua) to be one where people can be laughing so profusely with you but the very next minute they may be stabbing you. Of course, what is happening in Northern Nigeria, even as I speak, between Christians and Muslims, is not news that I need to be the one to break. And, third, the one seeking re-election with the nonsensical strategy was particularly from this Benin Kirbi area, the more reason for a person of the targeted class to be a sure victim there. Vahid might not have been able to see exactly why I was "chickening out" but as I have said many times before your therapy begins with you first understanding your situation.

The separation was not an easy one at all because Vahid and I had so much in common; being able to discuss academic and other issues very fruitfully despite our level gap. We had simply clicked in almost the same way Solo and I did in UNIYAO; but we finally were able to say goodbye and let go. My journey back home followed the same reversed course from Katsina Alla as the incoming trip; being kind of easier than the outward one – perhaps because I already had

113

the trekking experience; or simply because I was going to where I know and with someone there that was always in my thoughts. Just reaching Takum again where the trekking had to begin brought back a positive recollection of all the magical things that had happened from when I left Yoke in September 1981 till then. There were a lot of hard moments too but I was viewing all those only as blessings in disguise. I was returning to Yoke and farm work, for sure, and to start from scratch without money. But as I have said many times, money is not all that is necessary for success. If it were, then, surely the many lack of money situations, including the BIROCOL money palaver, should evidently have spelt the end of my road.

People sometimes talk about money in terms that would make you think happiness completely depends on the quantity of it that you have or spend. How much, for instance, did papa need to spend in 1981 to permit me enrol and study in the UNIYAO, compared to what he had until then used up on me? And compared to where the entire family would have been today? Again how much did I spend on the generator and other items that brought so much joy and celebration to Nwangong during my impromptu voyage in June 2004? Just about three hundred and fifty thousand francs CFA, which would be practically less than eight hundred Canadian dollars (about a month's rent in Montréal for a moderate 2-bedroom apartment). And I did not spend that amount of money simply because I had so much of it but because of my desire to make things better for the greatest number of persons possible. The one person (Anna) who almost entirely shared this perspective and with whom I wanted to work and walk throughout my life increasing "the greatest number of persons possible" was in Yoke to where I was then returning.

As a larger picture person, you hardly carry all your eggs in one basket as the many and diverse university admissions noted earlier can demonstrate. From Nkambe in the North West Region to Yoke in the South West Region (passing through the West and Littoral Regions), I made sure I was always occupying a seat by the window so that I could very quickly jot down postal information from the

114

sign boards of colleges as we passed by. Because I have very good sight and write extremely fast, I was able to note down many of them, including that of Collège de l'Unité de Manjo. Back to Yoke and farming, I did not consider it the end of the road just as it had not been after the Sasse re-admission saga. I regarded my being back there as a mere waiting period for the several teaching-position applications to bring up something with which to continue with the quest for university education after the 'wasted' but positively 'maturing' two academic years. But it looks like my being back in Yoke and to farming was interpreted by many (including the parents of my wife-to-be) as the final act; thus occasioning the events relating to Anna never becoming my wife. It is also amazing that Manjo would come calling only after (and not before) the Anna flop, a debacle that would seem to have catapulted the multiple disasters in the spouse quest (that I was until then no longer worrying about), crowned by the Scholastica surprising family definitional mess in Canada.

Chapter 4

Idealizing Marriage and Family: The Manjo Year, Yaoundé-Montreal effects, and Age Politics in University Education in Cameroon

It seems to me that people with the kind of outlook on life as mine often end up with the kind of marriage mess like mine because they idealize the institutions of marriage and of family in a world where self-centredness has become the rule rather than the exception; where take and take and take has long replaced give and take. When I talk about idealizing marriage and family, I am simply referring to three things at least; namely, (1) that both parties do share or learn to share the same or similar perspectives on as many domains as possible; (2) that both parents be there together to bring up the children and advance the family; and (3) that the marriage decision should begin with the two persons concerned. All the three requirements combine to bring about the ideal but sometimes only a few are present for a start, with the others being developed as the parties go along. I will examine particularly the third (which is like the gear-lever) in some details in the next chapter, drawing from my own case as well as from the intriguing experiences of other members of my large extended family. In this chapter, I dwell mostly on the duel and strategies of Manjo for getting to UNIYAO in time, with a slant on the Montreal positive that developed from a negative – CGAM – just like the information from God and/or divine intervention in Manjo.

The Manjo Duel and the Information from God

The town of Manjo is very critical to my UNIYAO bid; a longing that was being timed-out by the age-limit bar for university enrolment in Cameroon. The town is also very intimately tied to the second signification of "idealizing marriage and family", namely, that both parents should be there to bring up the children. These two principal considerations, exacerbated by the Anna-fiasco, created a real duel for me there, turning the year into a make-or-break one. Although "being there" is not just physical presence, the fact that I hardly know my birth father long led me to vow never to leave my own children with a similar "legacy". This could explain why I actually started wanting to have children only when I thought I was ready to be there (in all its forms) all the time for them. But, regrettably, it seems that the unwanted birth-father legacy is exactly what my kids are headed for even as (unlike my biological father) I am not yet dead; all this because of my failure to avoid having a narrow-minded spouse like papa had – thanks very much also to Yaoundé, the short-cut to which was also unnecessarily elongated. All these issues and more are interlocking and hidden in the Manjo brain-busting year.

Contrary to the thinking of a lot of people there, my one academic year in Manjo was not the bed of roses and of charming girls. Most people that knew me in that small town would find it hard to believe my realities in Manjo just as some others would to my realities in Canada. Because I have learnt not to carry my problems on my face, even the Manjo students themselves would find it hard to believe that I then had some real and devastating issues that were constantly with me. The greatest of them that almost tilted the balance against my returning to Cameroon, and which guided my approach to all the others in Manjo, was that of how to get to the UNIYAO the following academic year before the twenty-five year age-limit condition could bar me. I necessarily had to get enrolled in the UNIYAO by 1984 or never do so since thereafter I was to be twenty-five and above (things have changed today, of course). How was I to meet with this objective?

Yaoundé and my objectives are so connected that the city has undoubtedly also played a very significant role in my spouse quest for a number of reasons. First of all, could it not be that the Anna-fiasco that has so predominantly been at the centre of that quest was avoidable but for the nasty experiences I had had arriving Yaoundé

118

for the first time that then prevented me from enrolling in the University? Second, the earnest desire to pursue studies at the UNIYAO (the only university then in Cameroon) has had to mean my scrupulously avoiding anything that stood in the way of this longing. Could this not have also caused me to lose a very suitable wife in Manjo? And, third, in Yaoundé I was more ready than before, financially and otherwise, to assume family responsibilities; yet, it is in Yaoundé that some of my far-reaching and near-inexplicable spouse-quest gaffes happened.

Indeed the fiasco with Anna was so central to the transformation of the Manjo year into a real duel because she had been such a pillar of force for me since CCAS Kumba that the mere fact of knowing that I did not have her with/by me anymore (and through no real fault of ours) was actually a big drain on me and, therefore, on the combats and strategies for UNIYAO and life generally. The Manjo combats and strategies are so intimately interwoven (and also knotted to the Montreal effect) to the extent of being inseparable; but I have tried to tear them apart just for convenience and manageability, having to examine some of the roadblocks to the strategies for UNIYAO from the backstabbers. In Collège de l'Unité de Manjo I was on a salary of thirty-five thousand (35,000) francs CFA per month and it was obvious that with just that UNIYAO was kind of receding from view. To ensure that I did not have to spend more than one year in Manjo before enrolling in the UNIYAO, I tried to acquire as many teaching opportunities; and this, as far as Nkongsamba and Loum, with Manjo being the mid-point between the two. Apparently, backstabbers are gratuitously following and eating with me everywhere and every day.

Mr. Bangwa-man and Other Backstabbers

Inside Manjo itself, I had great chances with the only other semi-private secondary school called Collège Nlonako. One Bangwa man I met in Manjo was the senior English tutor there and it was to him that the Nlonako administration obviously turned for aid as to my

119

employability since they do not quite understand Anglophone certificates. Even Collège de l'Unité had to seek the views of the junior English tutor (John Teupuoh, from North West Region) before finalizing my hiring. At Collège Nlonako, Mr. Bangwa-man (I will prefer to call him like this) just did not want the man he calls all over town "my brother" to be anywhere near Nlonako; so he told the college administration that my certificates were fake, this message also being passed on to the principal of Collège de l'Unité who then tried to threaten me with exposure. Because of "my brother", I was never hired by Collège Nlonako despite that I and my teaching style had already become the talk of the day in and around Manjo. I do not usually go around nosing for information about people; but whenever having that information about them is essential to have in order to aid me in treading carefully it often miraculously comes to me. The information from God is what I have called it here. The cases of my brother Bernard in BIROCOL who led us to my parents-in-law are already behind us. I will give you just a few other instances out of a lot of them; these regarding, my very good friend's wife, including my own wife's mother again, and then back to Mr. Bangwa-man,

Solo's spouse is one of the only women to whom I would have easily sent my own wife for some marital schooling in view of the high esteem I hold both her and husband for being role models in many domains, including marriage and family. In 2006 Solo visited Canada to attend a conference at the International Civil Aviation Organization (ICAO) in Montréal and was putting up with me. On arrival he was so excited to tell me how my mother-in-law was putting up at his residence in Yaoundé and preparing for her visa to Canada. The way he was saying it told me that he must have been in the dark about a lot of what was going on under his roof. I merely informed Solo that I was hearing about it from him but it was so hard for him to believe that I was serious. Of course, he is my very good friend; but it is not in my way to call everyone in Cameroon and elsewhere to talk about what was/is going on in my family in Montreal. We moved on to other issues and my friend ate, slept and rested well.

120

Solo later called his home in Yaoundé to greet and let the family know he had arrived safely and indicating that he was at my home. He was then shocked to hear his own wife confidentially telling him not to let me know about Scholastica's mother being in Yaoundé because Scholastica does not want me to know. "Power, so you were serious when you said you did not know about it! My wife has just been telling me on the phone not to let you know about Scholastica's mother's trip to Yaoundé and I objected. How could Alice of all people on earth do such a thing?" I merely told Solo that I was just as bewildered as he was. No one is here saying that Alice should not help these people that she knows through me. But the fact that she joins the chorus that makes it look like I am such a bad person that would spoil the woman's trip to Canada makes me wonder if it is not the synonym of stabbing someone you are in front calling friend in the back. That attitude itself cannot be differentiated from the 'take and take and take' comportment of the wife I have spent the better part of my life moulding and improving through surmounting obstacles like those here in Manjo – being as well the handiwork of people who see only take and take and take as the rule in life. Is Scholastica's behaviour any different from Mr. Bangwa-man's calling me all over town "my brother" but telling Collège Nlonako not to hire me because my certificates are forged? Are marriage and family not to be defined by trust and truthfulness and upfront dealings?

I only had an idea of what must have happened in Collège Nlonako after I had stopped in Douala (to see Uncle Ngufor) on my way to Victoria for Christmas holiday of December 1983. I cannot exactly recall how the discussion led to Mr. Bangwa-man but I think my uncle asked if I had met any of our tribesmen in Manjo. When I mentioned his real names (as he was known in Manjo), Uncle Ngufor could not believe what he was hearing; explaining that the real owner of the names was long dead and that the person at the time in Manjo (whose actual names my uncle gave) was merely using the dead man's (Advanced Level) certificates and passing as him, concluding that the phony guy "does not even have the First School Leaving Certificate." I was not at all surprised by the revelation because I used to wonder a lot just listening to Mr. Bangwa-man's language. Now, just imagine Mr. Bangwa-man's lot if I were the vindictive type. This information from my uncle was however timely and very helpful for two especial reasons. First, I was then able to clearly see where and how the fake certificates story in Collège de l'Unité de Manjo had emanated; and, second, without this information, I should have been going to the devil for help regarding a second-term pregnancy issue (another worrisome Manjo roadblock), a thing which would simply have been like jumping from the frying pan to fire. Like the CCAS Kumba and other detractors, Mr. Bangwaman thus closed the Collège Nlonako 'quick door' to UNIYAO but my way of doing things helped out. Anything I do that would directly or indirectly bring more happiness to the greatest number of persons possible I do with excellence; even if it means pioneering it, like the creation of the CGAM that resulted from a negative answer to a restaurant.

Positive Out of Negative: Cameroon Goodwill Association of Montreal (CGAM)

As a larger picture person, I would say Scholastica is one of the brains behind the CGAM; not only because she was one of the thirteen founders but also largely because of her myopic refusal to run a restaurant despite the suggestion from many, including me. Many in the community wanted a point where they could be meeting regularly for good Cameroon-type food and socializing and Scholastica's restaurant seemed the perfect place because her cooking compares to none. It had become habitual for her dishes to vanish before the food of any other could be touched in gatherings. Her refusal was myopic or narrow-minded since she saw only her going to school and thereafter getting "a good job" as the singular way "to be able to help my brothers, sisters, and parents." That pushed open-minded and farsighted persons like me to look for other means of reaching the same or even bigger goals.

When the CGAM was created in July 2003, about nine of the thirteen founding members were Bangwa. It would have been so easy (as some of them were even hotly suggesting) to simply form a version of the home Bangwa meeting in Montreal. That was just too limiting because, as far as I was concerned, the capital idea behind the CGAM project was to especially provide 'soft landing' (something I myself never got on arriving in Montréal) to as many Cameroonians as possible that were coming into Canada generally and to Montréal (the entry port) in particular. Even though created by English-speaking Cameroonians, it was also not limited to that community but extended to every "Cameroonian of goodwill" and anyone having Cameroon familial connection, by marriage or adoption. Goodwill Montreal went places, setting the bar in community activities, with previously existing ethnic groupings (of East or French Cameroonian origin) copying its statutes and constitution that provided for extensive "social packages" to members and the community at large. These "social packages" included things like financial aid and moral support to those who: are bereaved, get married, are blessed with births, fall sick for a protracted period, etc.

But all these go-ahead projects began dropping when small-mindedness set in with the multiple creations of small village groupings from West of the Mungo River ('Anglophone Cameroon'), a process that was spearheaded especially by Lebialem or Bangwa. Imagine that in 2007 a CGAM founding member was nominated to run for the presidency of the CGAM but he turned it down, justifying his refusal on the lack of time etc. Thereafter he immediately went and formed the Lebialem Cultural and Development Association (LECDA) Montreal, being its first president. Other ethnic groups followed suit. The amazing thing is that all these mini-groups have simply taken the documents of the CGAM and replaced CGAM with their various appellations and then most of their membership come to the CGAM and argue against the continued availability of the social and other packages that they maintain in their ethnic mini-associations.

I truly tend to dislike small-mindedness; although I still work hand in hand with small-minded people. I do not need to belabour the point by saying that I would not be where I am today if I did not learn very early to do so. Of course, I have learned to dislike lies without disliking the one telling them; but some people tell lies so much that they become the embodiment of lies; making it hard to see how in such circumstances you can actually detest lies without disliking the person. When you have objectives in life like mine, you learn to dislike people's ideas; not the people themselves, because they are enclosed in "the greatest number of persons possible" that you want to ameliorate things for. Of course, a lot of short-sighted minds would be wondering why I did not react differently to the scheming comportment of my wife and her parents. Farsighted ones would know that it is because I am not like them. As already noted in the CCAS Kumba case, confronting narrow-mindedness with the same can never get you anywhere away from it. Because of my life objective, looking at the larger picture has largely been the driving force behind all of what I do (including those in regard of Scholastica *et al*), as it is behind the CGAM and other projects that I also pioneered.

I have often seen many persons with whom I had heatedly disagreed (say, during CGAM meetings) express surprise when I later say hello to them. This is usually because most of them fail to see that my disagreement with their idea expressed during those discussions has nothing to do with their person or character. They sort of fail then to see the larger picture, namely, that my disaccord with their postulated idea might actually be intended to make the Association even better so that more and more persons (including them) could benefit from the amelioration. Most of the points being made would be better understood, for instance, from the following proposals I made in the CGAM Forum at 1.36 PM on 19 November 2006, titled "My Idea of A Cameroon Goodwill Association of Montreal (CGAM) End of Year of Year Fund-raising Party: Suggestions" in which I stated or argued:

Hello Goodwillers, Let me salute you all with this idea of mine that no idea that is aired is useless. What I think is unfruitful is an idea that is not aired or made known. Sometimes (if not

124

often) it takes a small or little idea from one head to provoke or nourish a grand or big idea from another head. So, fellow Goodwillers, never think that your idea regarding how our dear CGAM could be made even grander (or on any issue whatever) is not big or important enough to be aired.

Of course, not all ideas that are aired would end up being acceptable to all and sundry. But that is quite a different matter from saying that only ideas that are to be acceptable should be put forward. By the way, how on earth are we to know whether or not an idea is to be welcomed favourably except by actually tendering it?

It is only normal for an association that has distinguished itself the way our CGAM has, to organize an end of year party. It is even more crucial when such a party is fund-raising inclined. It seems to me, from the lengthy discussions during our last CGAM meeting of 11 November 2006 that we have collectively missed a lot of things regarding the specifics of the type of party we are planning for the 30th of December this year. There are other pertinent issues that I would like us to review with the view of rendering CGAM even more effective in attaining its noble objectives. While touching upon some of these concerns here, I would like to anchor everything on and around our end of year fund-raising party.

1. The Party Organizing Committee (POC)

That the General Assembly of CGAM found the organization of this party very important in its bid to have finances available for the accomplishment of its goals, can be evidenced by its Resolution that also gave birth to the Party Organizing Committee (POC). Here are some recommendations in regard of this POC. First, let us make this POC a permanent organ of CGAM. By 'permanent' here, I simply mean to say that the POC should be an all-year-round functional body that shall be responsible for the organization (in liaison with the host, of course) of all CGAM parties (such as born-houses, baby-showers, marriages, meeting-hosting, Children Christmas, etc), including – but not limited to – the grand end of year one. Second, the POC should have mandate at such functions to take stock to ensure that members honour their responsibility (such as paying the required dues, bringing along a reasonable quantity of food or drinks, as the case may be) so as to make the occasion at hand the success that every CGAM event ought to be.

Third, this POC should be able to return to the venue of such ceremony, on the matter-of-course invitation of the host, and collect all returnable bottles (I can already see some of you laughing here, but wait a minute) and exchange them for the cash that the treasurer will put in what I will like to characterize here as the End of Year Party Fund (see #2 below). Just imagine (conservatively) that there are a hundred of such bottles after every CGAM event or party and then do the arithmetic for yourselves, considering en plus the regularity of such events within the CGAM circle. This is just one of the myriad of very efficacious means of raising funds to facilitate the realization of some, if not all, of our well-intentioned goals and objectives while at the same time sparing members of the need to contribute – at that time of the year when, as we all know, the financial pressure from back home is at its peak – toward the organization of the end of year party.

2. The End Of Year Fund-Raising Party Fund (EYFPF)

Let us give Goodwillers a break in the usual all-year-round contributions to this and that. Let us strive for means to make CGAM and Goodwillers mutually respectful of each other. I am therefore suggesting here that we create the EYFPF similar to what we now have as the Emergency Fund (see #4 below). Every member (new and old) should be required to pay the totality of these two Funds before their admission or renewal of membership at the date of application or in

January of every year, as the case may be. Since this might be coming very close to the January line, it could be that we make an exception for 2007 (should we decide to institute it) and extend the deadline to about March for the January Option (old members). Of course, this will apparently be burdensome initially and at first look. But the institution of this EYFPF will not only free most of us from the aforementioned peak period financial pressures. It will also ensure that our POC can strategically plan for and organize the grand party and, consequently, we will be able to generate more resources that can enable the speedy realization, for example, of our dream of having our own hall and meeting venue. A typical explication will suffice here. With the funds readily available at the beginning of the year, the POC can (whenever it finds beer, wine, and other liquours on sale) buy large quantities of them and stock. It can as well use this stock of drinks to generate more funds even before the grand party by reselling (at a little less than the current prices but more than its purchase price) to any Goodwiller who is organizing a little or big "something".

Goodwillers, let us look around us and try to see what we have so far not been seeing, not because we cannot see but simply because we refuse to see what we should see. Only the sky will be the limit to us if we not only pool our resources together but also think big and open our eyes wide enough to perceive what is going on around us. Not to sound like belittling the fun-having side of CGAM, I was amazed by the amount of dollars that our last financial report indicated we had spent for just entertainment alone. Amazed because, for almost the same length of time in its operation some years back, the defunct Cameroon Investment Club (CamInvest) could not raise up to five thousand dollars ($5000.00). It had degenerated so much into a "Big-Talking" Club rather [than] an Investment Club that its spontaneous death came as no surprise to some of us that had

127

become so disillusioned by the wrong direction the Club was taking. Maybe the time is now right to reinvent something in the nature of CamInvest? There is nothing that stops CGAM and CamInvest (if we care about its rebirth) from going along hand in hand.

3. CGAM's Non-Profit Status

This hyphenated status has been raised, on countless occasions, to stop CGAM from levying one or other interest rate on its generous loans to its members. We must henceforth desist from burning our candles from both ends. This notorious argument has led several members of CGAM to stop participating in the savings part (a very crucial part) of CGAM and the result we all know: empty bank account whenever a member desperately requires a loan. It is not surprising. No one will need to be an academic economist to comprehend that the very idea of savings imports that of interest returns. The higher the rate of interest returns, the greater the motivation for people to save their money and the easier it also becomes for those in dire need of the loans to get them. It is a win-win situation and should remain that way: Say goodbye to the hyphenated word argument for another reason.

The proponents of this hyphenated status theory have often indicated that CGAM cannot charge a higher rate of interest because it is a non-profit organization as per its by-laws or constitution. If we have to stick to this definition of non-profit association, then there will be no need for any interest rate at all, whether 5% or 0.0005%. No non-profit organization, I believe, could function if that were the right description to be attached to it. True to say that CGAM is a non-profit association. But, quote me anywhere at any time if you like, a non-profit organization is not prohibited from raising funds to meet its objectives. It is rather proscribed from being solely profit-making inclined. How, for example, is CGAM going to "promote socio-economic and cultural values" of its members without the financial means to do so? If CGAM were to raise enough funds today to be able to purchase some apartment buildings from which it[] gets money (in the form of rents and tax returns) with which it fosters solidarity between, and easier integration of, members of its community, would CGAM have ceased to be a non-profit association and become a profit-making organization?

Brothers and sisters, let me seize the opportunity here to tell you that the objectives of CGAM are broad and extensive enough to allow us the legal leeway to do the things that we intend to do. To be able to do these things, we need money; and to get this required money we need to do a lot of things. All these things we can simply not be able to do, or even attempt doing, if we let Mr. Timidity take the better part of us. We must have to put ourselves in a position that is comfortable enough to easily confront events before us, be they planned and long-awaited such as births and other joyful occasions or emergencies such as deaths and other crippling accidents.

4. The Emergency Fund

There has been a stark difficulty with this Fund this year, contrary to expectations. Why? There may be several causes but I will tell you one thing that is for sure. We have rapidly been using this Fund very inappropriately. That is to say that we have developed this odd habit of employing this Fund to things that are anywhere but near emergency. I do not think that births and marriages, for instance, are emergencies. Let us henceforth strictly restrict the dipping of hands into this Fund for emergencies. The birth of a baby into our CGAM Family is not an emergency, no matter how largely we try to expand that notion. We can generally prepare well in advance to dip our hands into our respective pockets toward this event, especially after the Baby-Shower (if there is one) or the traditional announcement of delivery. After such breaking of the good news

129

via e-mail, what we should be doing (rather than filling the group website with myriad of congratulatory messages) is to see the Treasurer/POC and pay the stipulated amount of contribution needed for the born-house. This is what we should do while sending the congratulations to or through the couple's private e-mail address or phone that we all have. The same goes for marriages and others.

Fellow Goodwillers, the CGAM has, within its short period of existence, attained heights that are yet to be reached by similar very long-standing associations of Cameroonian colourings. This is largely due to the fact, as Mr. Martin Mpana [then Cameroon Acting High Commissioner in Ottawa] rightly put it [during their Recognition and Honouring event by CGAM], that we are very well organized. I will here implore that we do not limit our renowned organizational ability to receptions and parties but carry it (through those) to the 'Outer Limits' of investment and business. In view of CGAM's status within our larger community, our End of Year F. Party, if very well planned and organized, can provide us the Gateway to the "Outer Limits".

Thank you for your time. Long Live CGAM!

These are suggestions based on a larger-picture view of things that would scarcely be adequately grasped by small-mindedness. Narrow-mindedness will obviously preclude you from serving in any capacity in the administration of your successor. That is totally out of the question when you have objectives that are grounded in the larger picture and by which you define yourself. Of course, it works both ways; because as open-minded as you may be, it would be impracticable to serve in your successor's administration if he or she is not also as open-minded; which is almost similar to the same problems you will encounter working "hand out of hand" with your spouse who looks only at the narrow picture and defines family through scheming.

The world would surely be a better place if people generally look at the larger picture. It is the larger picture persons that, as the

CGAM presidents, have left some positive milestones in the history of the association. Paul Ayah took over from me and carried the CGAM to a different and unprecedented level; largely using the internet in its management and operation, the scope of the association also being enlarged and modernized. I vividly recall how his progressive proposal for CGAM recognition and honouring of some diplomats at the Cameroon High Commission in Ottawa met with stiff opposition from the bulk of the members, most of who could not then look at the larger picture and accused him of using the CGAM for his post-hunting in Cameroon. Disagreeing with someone's idea is one thing and libelling them is another and the line had obviously been crossed. Paul came around swinging when he gave CGAM a bit of his impressive curriculum vitae in a subsequent meeting. It appears that many that had been going around with the stupid suggestion had not done their homework to know exactly with whom they were dealing because thereafter the opposition had a glimpse of the larger picture Paul was eyeing. After serving for the two terms maximum permitted by the CGAM constitution, he handed over in January 2007 to Hans Najeme.

It had become almost given that each president served the two terms permitted as they were usually returned to office unopposed. That was not the case with the Najeme administration. An open-minded person hardly respects a tradition that is not progressive. The Najeme administration seems to have indulged in what is now known as the Pepper Soup and Heineken Syndrome; draining the CGAM coffers dry; and generally not paying attention to what the general membership was saying. Fidelis Folefac was obviously settled on replacing Najeme after the first term and to once more bring honour to the CGAM. He planned far ahead by astutely recruiting a lot of members from his Bangwa community into CGAM. Najeme on the contrary failed to look ahead to see the approaching storm despite that Dr. Folefac (as he now is) had made it clear to him that he (Folefac) was bent on butting him out of office in the following elections period, naively believing in the traditional return for a second term.

November 2007 saw another milestone in the CGAM's history with the crushing thrashing of Najeme and the rise of the exceptional phenomenon called Fidelis Folifac. CGAM moved yet to another level under this gentleman's presidency, revamped and fortified with the unprecedented visibility in the LaSalle Borough that the Association thereafter acquired. In short, Dr. Folefac's community engagement through CGAM earned him the Moulin d'Or Prize from the LaSalle Borough. The new bar set by Dr. Folefac has practically made it very hard for those following him successively (Edward Takang, Florence Nankam, Ignatius Mbeng) to really shine in the spot, despite their various efforts to stay away from the Najeme Administration's syndrome and to make CGAM better and better. Caren Ayah is the current CGAM president, having assumed office in January 2013. Positive CGAM resulted from a negative answer to a restaurant; just as providence had its unique way of readjusting Mr. Bangwa-man's negative-backstabbing balance through Unexpected Dividends of Teaching Excellence in Manjo.

The Unexpected Dividends of Teaching Excellence: Divine Intervention?

"I have fallen for you not because you are teaching English but I am sure your way of teaching it has made many of us to come to like the subject." This is a Manjo female student's thesis from a conversation I had with her. Her truthful postulation during that enamoured conversation immediately reminded me of my first economics tutor in Sasse College who we nicknamed *Gentlemen* because almost every phrase or sentence from Mr. Etta began with the word. I certainly defied pigeonholing into sciences or arts but I fell in love with economics (taught from form three) because of the way *Gentlemen* introduced the course to us. "Gentlemen, six blind men went to see the elephant. The first approached from the side and shouted 'I have seen the elephant, it's like a wall; the second, from the ear, said it is like a leaf; the third, from the tail described it as a rope;... Now, Gentlemen, which of the six blind men actually saw the

132

elephant?" As we were all happily and noisily debating the answer, *Gentlemen* cut in with "Gentlemen, as you can clearly see, all of them saw the elephant but none of them saw it intact. Gentlemen, economics is like the elephant...." That was extremely captivating for an introduction to the subject; an appeal which rightly, in my view then, deserved my paying great attention to *Gentlemen* in order to visualize this 'Elephant' intact.

Yes, a teacher's presentation of the subject, especially in the first few days, matters a lot; and the Manjo student was indeed quite right and truthful. She was not just speaking from the standpoint of someone who was so deeply in love with the senior English tutor in Collège de l'Unité de Manjo. Quite apart from being Mr. English, I am someone that does not usually get into doing a thing unless I intend to do it to the best of my abilities. At the UNIYAO my tutorial classes were always jammed with non-group students who came to imbibe the "stuff" dished out in a way not common in the milieu. At the UNIBU (University of Buea), my law of tort lectures were often attended by non-law students; most of them coming to "*chop* Christmas with my own eyes" (that is, see and hear for themselves). Teaching is a thing that comes so naturally with me; but it is not the only thing I do well.

Second term in Manjo changed the dynamics of almost everything. I remember fondly the drastic cuts in my monthly expenditures after the first term holiday. It is January 1984 I am talking about here. Most Manjo parents were not willing to sell anything anymore to "Teacher" (that is the way they called me). Why? The stories are endless but one or two will suffice here. On the first market day after Christmas holiday I was there to get the usual foodstuff and other items. A mother from whom I usually bought a bucket of Igbo cocoyam already had a bag waiting when I approached her shed. She handed over the bag but refused to take payment. Three or four sheds away a father shouted: "Teacher, don't forget to come for your packet of beans; it is ready." It was like every parent in the market already had what I usually bought from them

133

waiting for pickup; every one of them similarly refusing to take payment.

As the cocoyam mother joyfully explained, her son had had to write the *Brevet* (BEPC) four times without success. (Now, also begin to visualize this coupling with the university-entering age-limit nonsense then in Cameroon!) But he had come home one day and very excitedly told them that he was having that certificate that academic year (1983-84) because of his new English teacher who had arrived a few weeks before; the tangible evidence being also in his first term results in which he had an overall average (*moyen général*) of 10.5 on 20. Therefore, the mother had concluded, "when I say I am not taking money from you for the cocoyam, it is my way of saying thank you very much for the good work you are doing for the future of our children." When I tried to explain that I am already being remunerated for the "good work" and did not need to be paid twice for the same job, I got an eye-opener when she retorted: "Who said I was paying you? I simply said I was showing my appreciation." Wow!

"Teacher," yet another voice cut in, "please, don't you tell us not to appreciate your marvellous job because the college is paying you. Was the college not also paying those who were there before you but not helping our children the way you are doing? As for me, I am not selling but buying; I would however like to invite you to come and have lunch with us because my daughter is so certain of making her *brevet* this school year and has since been speaking only English to us at home. For the first time, she has had an overall average of 11 on 20 in an exam, telling us that English that has this far been her greatest nightmare is now within her control." Both of those students were right indeed because I understood the problem well and tackled it as well with innovative techniques.

Knowing and Mastering the Problem

In Cameroon's French-speaking educational system students do not pass in examinations by minimum number of subjects passed in with the minimum score as the English-speaking system warrants. As

Anyangwe (1989: 199 n.6) duly explained it about five years after my Manjo stay, "One contrast between the *Brevet* and *Bac* examinations on the one hand, and the G.C.E. O' & A' Level examinations, on the other hand, is that in the former, in order to obtain a certificate the candidate need only score an average of 50% on the aggregate of the marks for the subjects taken; whereas in the G.C.E. he must score at least 50% in each of the required number of subjects." Having taught in both 'systems' of education in Cameroon for a couple of years, I have had several opportunities to listen to French-speaking students' admiration and yearning for the "*système anglophone*".[12] But they are condemned to live with what they do not like simply because parochialism on the part of the leaders would not permit 'copying' from *la minorité*, in spite of the great harm that not doing so brings to young French-speaking Cameroonians.

There is no doubt that disciplines like English, French, and mathematics are compulsory in both educational systems. But a student can still easily make the G.C.E. certificate without *all* of these compulsory subjects. For example, my brother Joseph made his G.C.E. at both levels, although he could not register in the UNIYAO because he did not have any of the three. The important thing though is that he obtained his certificate with which he moved on to further study in the USA. This is not the case with the *Bac et al* methodology where there is a pronounced debilitating handicap that the authorities perpetuate without *seeming* to realize. The compulsory English language subject alone, for instance, could and is well known (from the two students just noted above) to stand in the way of most Francophone students for years, through dragging down their *moyen général*. As the politics in place also does not encourage these French-speaking students to consider English and anything associated with it as important, that system of education then kind of imprisons most of its students. The English language-reducing-*moyen général* thesis being criticized here could duly explicate why most of these

---

[12]For more detailed critical studies on Cameroon's two systems of education, see Fossungu (2013a: 175-192, 90-110, & 45-59).

135

Cameroonian French-speaking students do prefer to cross to neighbouring French-speaking countries (Central African Republic, Chad, Congo, and Gabon) to take the *Baccalauréat* examinations there. Dr. Christopher Nsahlai, Cameroon's ambassador to the first of these neighbouring countries, clearly made the point on the mass border crossings in an interview in 1996.[13] Understanding the problem is easily solving it.

Some Methods Employed for Diagnosis: Teaching English in English

My task then in Manjo (as well as in Institut d'Études Commerciales MATAMFEN in Yaoundé, etc) was to aid these students to score not less than an eight on twenty in English; and to accomplish it, I devised lots of unique teaching techniques that were wholly revolutionary. Ground-breaking in the sense that students began skipping other favourite courses in order to *voler les cours d'Anglais* (attend my English language lessons not normally scheduled for them). The techniques included things such as putting some salient distinctions (e.g. hard & had; walk & work; thought & taught; were & where) in class-beginning songs. An example is this one (the chorus being general/constant to all the songs):

As John was *walking* to school this morning, his head was *working*
Because he *thought* all along about what the teacher *taught* in class yesterday
Until he got to *where* the other students *were* assembled
And told them English was not as *hard* as he *had* imagined
Chorus: I love my English lessons and I am going to pass my exams this year

---

[13] See "I Am Not an Absent Ambassador – Nsahlai" *The Herald* N° 322 (24-26 June 1996), 6.

It is not just my teaching style that makes me a successful and well-liked teacher. One of my early primary school-acquired separation-balancing skills also plays a very noteworthy role; as well as my refusal to teach the English language in French. The application of that induced separation-balance/cooperation of matters of the heart and academics has not been limited to my own student years (male student-female student relations) but extends as well to my relations with those I teach. With me, the only advantage my student girlfriend, for example, has over the other students is the fact that I am available 24/24 and 7/7 to explain or answer questions on anything she does not understand; but never to accord her undeserved marks. My Manjo student girlfriend was so very special to me and when she said she did not fall for me because I was teaching English she was very serious. She shared this same philosophy, as many of my other perspectives, to the extent that I sometimes wondered if she was not my younger identical twin-sister.

This separation-balancing skill in teaching has proven to be one of my strongest forces in the domain, setting me apart from the "marks scewers" and "money harvesters,"[14] and winning the trust and admiration of both male and female students. I vividly recall the hullabaloo that went around when my sister Marie-Claire failed the tort law examination that I graded at the UNIYAO; and also when my wife's best friend (that many in the UNIBU mistook for my lover) failed the same when I taught there. Many just could not figure out how that can be normal in an environment where the twisted is

---

[14]One education critic in 1998 told the story of the "non-doctorate doctors [in the UNIYAO who] work as a team", one of whom "boasted around Bonamoussadi [the student residential quarters] saying, 'I have the fate of 300 students in my hands' and in this position, he collected ten thousand [CFA] frs. (10,000) from each student who wanted a score of 12 and above on 20. Shame! You probably heard of this other one who, given the chance to scrutinize the files of freshmen for admission, admitted students who had neither French nor English – a prerequisite for admission. It was not an error. He did this by harvesting twenty-five thousand francs from each of the students who lacked this criterion." Shey Sheradin, "Ngoa-Ekele Doctors without Doctorate Degrees" *The Herald* (Cameroon) (2-3 December 1998), 10.

the norm (should I say 'like father like son'?); with no one bringing this incomprehension out as well as a student in the UNIYAO that I briefly dated.

Rosemary came home one day after test papers had been distributed and she did not score well. She was very respectful as usual in public, never addressing me by my first name but by "Sir" (and "Dear" in private). But not so on that day. "Peter, I cannot believe that you failed me in the test. What's the matter with you...?" I had to cut her short, making things as clear as they should be. First, I told her, "I do not fail any student; if others do that, it is not my way. You fail because you do not merit passing. Second, you should be asking what the matter is with you, not with me." Rosemary was certainly not taking it in when she asked: "Why then am I your lover? What for, Peter?" I looked at her angry face for about two minutes (wondering why my Manjo girlfriend could not be there at that very moment to address her for me) before telling her to tell me when her anger was gone so that I could then respond to her queries.

When Rosemary told me she was ready, I demanded if she had just dropped into town when she decided to go out with me. She said no. "Then you must have at least had an idea of who I was, or didn't you?" I asked. As she was saying nothing, I added: "Has someone sent you to come and change me then?" It happened as if it were Sam's Mother hammering the truth nail into Sam because Rosemary startled and said "How did you know?" before trying to retract with "I mean how do you mean?" I did not press further except to pick on her first question which I interpreted to her as meaning in effect that she was a lover to all those lecturing courses she passed in. She left my home together with the relationship; but not with my teaching practice and principles that dated back as far as Ekondo-Titi, Bamenda, and especially Manjo where I also refused teaching English in French.

Another important tool I employed in Manjo (as elsewhere) was something that initially irritated most of the students – my firm refusal to teach English in French. It worked very well because many of them got the impression that I was null in French and thus began

138

struggling to express themselves in class only in English, with the opportunity of my correcting them as they went along. I recall the first few days in one class when a student put his hand up and was given permission to talk or ask a question. He instead made the following comments in French: "Our English teachers have always explained things to us in French. I don't know how you are going to teach us when you cannot speak French." I perfectly understood him but seized the opportunity to send a very clear message when I turned to the best English student in class to explain to me what he had just said. After the explanation, I addressed the entire class in English, of course:

Listen to me carefully. First, this is the first and last time anybody will act as translator in this class. Second, I am here to help you obtain your *brevet* and any of you who would pay attention to my English lessons can already consider that certificate yours this school year. I know what the problem is and working together we will fix it. That is what I have been hired to do; not to learn French at your expense like your former English teachers. Let those who want to have their brevet this school year put up their hands.

Everyone's hand was up. Collège de l'Unité de Manjo's brevet results were far better than previously and, when I returned there to teach in September 1984 in order to collect my holiday money, Collège Protestant de Ndoungué (near Nkongsamba) came knocking with a hefty job offer. The salary there (sixty thousand francs per month) was almost twice what I was making in Collège de l'Unité de Manjo; plus a big and spacious two bedroom house and other amenities. This was a mission institution with a high school section as well and I could also have combined its junior English tutor position with the Collège de l'Unité de Manjo position. But the call to university education was far too loud and pressing; the more so after what I had had to do to overcome Manjo's obstacles and other objectives clashes. I left for the UNIYAO. Some of the Yaoundé City

139

effects have been noted earlier. The additional fact is that I not only lived the longest in Yaoundé but also at a level I was ready to settle down, having enrolled for university education that had been haunting and hurting other family "settlement" issues. Why was family then not begun until about ten years after university enrolment? Could it be attributed to boldness and truthfulness and the marriage decision?

Chapter 5

Boldness, Truthfulness, and the Marriage Decision In Africa: Intriguing Responses From A Bangwa Royal Family

Boldness and truthfulness are two sides of the same coin and have undoubtedly been the most pronounced hallmarks of my fascination for any woman, lover or spouse. To be bold is simply not to be afraid to confront the truth. When you begin to make a distinction as to when to tell the truth, you become a liar because truthfulness knows no such distinction. Therefore, if you are not true to yourself, you cannot be bold; and, since truthfulness has no distinction, boldness also should not. As noted earlier, all three requirements of "idealizing marriage and family" combine to bring about the ideal but sometimes only a few are present for a start, with the others being developed as the parties go along. I will tackle the marriage decision as properly to be that of the two parties concerned. I think this requirement needs to be carefully examined because I am inclined to think that most of the problems already noted above would be excluded if the decision to marry each other "for better and for worse" was truly that of the two people concerned. This factor is studied under three main heads, namely, (1) whether boldness and truthfulness make 'ground-breaking unions' for 'virgin-ground breakers',(2) an analysis of some declarations made at a previous spouse quest, and(3) the marriage style and close-knit relations of writer's marriage.

Boldness, Truthfulness, and 'Ground-Breaking Unions'

Boldness and truthfulness are two sides of the same coin and I have realized from my own experiences that the few times that I have made the decried distinction (as to when to be bold) have led to colossal failures. If you know that you have to always stay bold and

141

true to yourself and live by it, you will not bother, for instance, to tell lies just to have relatives and/or friends support your marriage if the decision to get married is actually that of both of you. An apt example to the point, to begin leading you to my own stimulating case, comes from my sister Marie-Claire who embraced the truth in Chapter 1 and did not leave the household in Victoria; but she appears to be refusing to hug the truth while in America and consequently redefining family, as shown in the family hit parade of marrying in America.

Marrying in America

I guess Marie-Claire and her husband have never been able to live with the bitter truth; they have thus gotten themselves embroiled in situations that no truth lover would have gotten into. When I was leaving Cameroon in 1991 to Edmonton, Alberta, my sister handed me two letters addressed to two persons in the United States, one in New York City (NYC) and the other in the Washington DC area. In Edmonton, I got two bigger envelopes into which I put her letters including my phone contact for receipt confirmation. Both men called later to confirm; and regularly called thereafter to chat. Between when I finished my programme and graduation day, I wanted to visit the USA and, preferably, the DC area since I had heard that many of my Sasse College mates were there. I called the DC guy (later to be my sister's husband) but he gave excuses; whereas the NYC guy was so happy and enthusiastic to receive me and it was there that I went. I returned to Cameroon after my Alberta convocation ceremony in November 1992 and in early 1993 we were in the village (Nwangong) for Marie-Claire's traditional marriage rites. It seems that before I had arrived at the ceremony ground some members of the family had been having problems with the fact that no one in the family actually knew the suitor in the USA and Marie-Claire had said I did know him. Arriving and being asked, I made it clear that I had had the opportunity to talk to him several times on the phone but had never met him in person. Marie-Claire was

142

obviously not happy that I had not lied to cover up her own lie. Why did she even have to lie about the issue when no one was even saying she was not going to marry the guy until someone in the family in fact knew him?

Still in the domain, there was another man in New York with whom I (at the time in Montréal, Québec) had often been talking on the phone but never actually met. He was interested in (marrying) my cousin, Violet, and he called me one day to find out a lot of things about her. Believing that he has to do his homework by himself, as well as my stand on the truth, I told this man that I was not the right person to respond to his inquiries since I did not even grow up together with Violet and consequently do not know much of what he wanted to know. (And, frankly, I would have told Marie-Claire's husband the same thing, less the growing up portion, if he had called to ask the same about her: not being a police-like brother or nose poker.) This New York guy then called Cameroon and broadcast that Violet claims that I am her brother whereas I have denied ever knowing her. It became Number One on the family hit-parade echoes, with many seeing me as the one who had spoiled Violet's chances of marrying someone based in America, and, consequently, her own coming to America. In the meantime, someone who knew exactly who he was and what he wanted left North America to Cameroon to do whatever needed to be done to marry beautiful Violet. He and Violet were in Montréal for a while before relocating to Kentucky in the USA. Violet has not stopped thanking me for having stayed true to who I am because that has greatly helped her to "the real man" (her words) she now has as husband. That is part and parcel of what I mean by ameliorating the life of "the greatest number of persons possible", directly or indirectly.

On the contrary, I guess Marie-Claire and husband took my truthfulness for a sin against them; my deduction being solidly founded on the following facts. Her husband came to Cameroon in early 1994 and Scholastica and I gave him all the treats deserving of a brother-in-law, suspending our regular activities in order to drive him around as he visits other relations of his, public transportation being

143

what it is in Cameroon. When he was returning, I handed him my application to McGill University that was missing just the application fee of sixty dollars or 60$ (because it was then not possible to issue international money orders except to France). I even gave him the equivalent amount in francs CFA but he refused accepting the money, saying he would handle it. I never heard from the school although he claimed to have sent in the application. That can clearly not be true because whether it was complete or not the school must have communicated that information to me. When they get overseas, some of these people think people back home are so ignorant about how things work overseas; not even considering the fact that some people are back home now but have also lived for a long time overseas.

I missed that school year but did it again (including many others) and sent to my white friends in Edmonton (Andrew and Nancy Whistance-Smith) who completed all the applications with the required fees and sent. I got acknowledgement of receipt from all the concerned schools immediately. That is how I was able to get into McGill in 1995. Who would be denying that good friends are better bad or scheming family members? In addition, with the McGill programme completed in February 1997 (and viewing what can be described as Canada's stupid immigration regulations[15]), I visited my sister and brother-in-law in Bowie, Maryland, hoping to find my feet there in the USA but all I got was their behaving as if I had come there to babysit their daughter for them.

It is also amazing, since I am talking truthfulness and boldness and family, that Marie-Claire and husband could not see the need to

---

[15] For instance, job opportunities in my field (university lecturer or other positions in the public service generally and the professional guilds) are directed only to Canadian citizens and permanent residents; and to become a permanent resident, I would need to show that I have that job. That is for people like me who have already spent so much studying and living in Canada. But someone that has instead studied, say, in Belgium and wants to become a Canadian permanent resident is very advantageously welcomed, not being saddled with this roundabout exclusion that I had squarely tasted before graduating from McGill University in February 1997.

144

pick up Scholastica (their brother and brother-in-law's wife) at the airport in America when this same woman gave Marie-Claire's husband the treats mentioned earlier when he came to Cameroon. How soon the ungrateful types forget good deeds! Marie-Claire appears to have redefined family in America to include only her blood siblings, but not the 'brother' without whose guidance and other moral and financial support she would never have achieved anything in the household. Apart from her own definition not being un-African and un-American, there is not much difference (as far as concerns me) in her changing definition of family while in America and that of Scholastica while in Canada. One would have thought that Marie-Claire, of all people, would favour a much more inclusive definition of family, as well as develop a very long memory for good deeds.

If she never learnt this lesson while in the household, I am hoping that she has done so from Joseph's death in Dallas, Texas, in June 2007. When this occurred, I could only channel financial contribution (including my 'social packages' from CGAM or Goodwill Montreal) to Marie-Claire. But for the relentless effort of this smart woman (one of those 'children whose fathers have all died and they are here eating our father's money') Joseph's corpse would never have reached Cameroon. Marie-Claire actually accompanied the corpse home; with me not being able to even travel to Dallas since my passport was then suspended by Justice Canada because of outstanding child support arrears to Scholastica; the desired and inevitable result of her own definition of family. The good news though is that Joseph had a decent burial in his place of birth, thanks to his two "outsider" brother and sister in North America. I think humanity as a whole would benefit when we do not meet pettiness with parsimoniousness: You can continue and conclude by imagining what Mami Thecla's definition of family would have meant to her birth-child (Joseph) if Marie-Claire also did not listen to me and learn but instead left the household as desired.

Indicative that Marie-Claire has also learnt a lot from Joseph's demise is her chief title of Fofah (which literally means "Chief who

145

gives") bestowed on her in 2008 during the enthronement of Fon NN Fossungu. This is not something you see often and the total number of female chiefs in the entire Bangwa clan cannot be more than five. Furthermore, Fofah was in Montreal for the first time in May 2009, arriving from Maryland with her two daughters, two brothers, and mother for my traditional marriage ceremony. I can only be hopeful that we learn to find some positives in tragedies and also to embrace the truth without becoming bitter. Some of the things previously mentioned happen because a lot of people cannot live with the truth and thus become bitter when it is flung into their faces. Needless to say that is no excuse for the truth not to be told without distinguishing who or what is concerned and when. I will therefore continue to fling the truth into faces (including mine) with (1) First Tradition-Breakers and Success from Tragedy,(2) the Peter-Scholastica marriage decision, (3) the marriage quest declaration, and (4) marriage style, including closely-knit relations.

First Tradition-Breaker and Success from Tragedy

My belief is that serious relationships (leading to marriage) have to begin between the two people concerned before reaching their various families. Uncle Ngufor and I have seen eye to eye on several issues but this is one area where we have strongly disagreed. Justine, a Bangwa girl, was the wife Uncle Ngufor had slated for me during the post-Edmonton period. He is certainly someone whose indication in the matter would have received serious consideration from me but he never proposed or even discussed the matter with me before going ahead and making all his arrangements with Justine's parents. Even the girl's parents were kind of apprehensive and wondering if I would go along with the plan, with my uncle assuring them: "Don't worry. I know Peter very well; be rest assured that it would work because he can never refuse what I tell him to do." Indeed. I remember several occasions on which I visited Uncle Ngufor's home in (Quartier Non-Glacé in) Douala only to find Justine also entering on my heels and then almost everyone else at home suddenly disappearing, leaving just

146

the two of us. What kind of trap were they setting and to catch who? Justine was quite beautiful, quiet and amenable and seemed to be a very good girl for a wife but for the fact that she was allowing herself to be used in the way my uncle was doing. Obviously a girl that I would have taken a second look at if I met her on the way, I invited her one day to my cousin's home where I was then living in order to advise her to stop behaving the way she was doing. She came alright, heavily accompanied by her sister. What was going on, I thought to myself. What were they up to? That was the last time I set eyes on Justine.

Still in Douala, this time in 2007 and contrasting vividly with the Justine case, I visited another uncle when I returned from Nwangong via Bafut where I had met the parents and other relations of a lady I had talked marriage to. I had not even mentioned marriage to my uncle, let alone the intelligent nurse of the Nwangong health post, when he stated that he did not agree to my marrying her because, as he had earlier put it to Marie-Claire, she is "a woman that everyone in Nwangong has slept with." Marie-Claire's spontaneous response to him had been "Have you too [from Nwangong] slept with her?" Who should even be complaining about that here? I wonder why people just like poking their noses where they have no business. Did I even tell some of these people that I was about marrying the lady because she was still a virgin? That is how I ended the matter with my uncle and the likes of him but not with the lady, making me wonder greatly why this decision-condition was waived in my marriage to Scholastica, a marriage that is very unlike the others, including that of the 'first tradition-breaker'.

The two people concerned are those that have to matter a lot. I had gone to Bafut not to commence the decision with the intelligent nurse's parents but to let them meet the person that had proposed and their daughter had accepted to marry. This is because serious relationships that lead up to marriage have to begin between the two people concerned before reaching their various families. I learned this vital lesson at a very young age from Foletia, one of my several uncles who always make me marvel. Whenever Foletia opens his mouth to

147

talk, I am struck by his logical sequence, wisdom, sense of purpose, flow, and what have you, and I can only compare his giftedness in the field to Uncle Ntimah's.

Foletia is the one who, for the very first time (as far as I know), openly "disobeyed" my grandpa, Fon ST Fossungu, on the question of his marrying who he (Foletia) wanted and not the choice of the family. Foletia met his wife in Mbonge (near Kumba) where he was teaching but the Fon refused his marrying the woman probably because she is not Bangwa. Foletia fearlessly and firmly stood his grounds with his Bameleke wife-to-be and did not capitulate despite the long duration of the 'war'. Foletia eventually triumphed; getting his wife who, living in Nwangong since, has become a model wife and exemplary mother to all and sundry; also making her husband one of the most successful and happily married in the royal family. Foletia's example is clearly one of boldness and truthfulness in regard of what one is after; also being, without a doubt, indicative of the fact that the two people marrying or about to should be able to make the initial decision, with the rest of their extended families merely supporting them. Foletia' stance contrasts very vividly with a lot of other uncles and aunts that allowed (outdated) tradition to unnecessarily rule and ruin them in the matter.

This is not to say however that following tradition in the matter has always been catastrophic in the family; the proof being in Aunty Elizabeth Nzouata Fossungu's marriage. While the initial decision criterion is essential, the capacity of the parties to subsequently develop or learn to cultivate commonality of priorities can supersede all else. Is this realization what must have influenced Peter's minimising of the initial decision factor in his marriage to Scholastica? In brief, I am talking about being bold and truthful in sticking to who you are and what you want. Aunty Nzouata's success story began from my sister's tragedy and marriage. I am referring to Therese who papa had dumped in the village after the Pepper Incident in Yoke.

Therese was of course not the village-staying type but, without money, had no means of leaving and coming back to *ncheng* or the

148

coast. One day the opportunity came knocking and begging on her doorsteps in the person of a labourer with the Cameroon Development Corporation (CDC) who was living in a CDC camp in the Meanja Rubber Estate, Muyuka. Vincent Nkengafac, the person concerned, was generally known to us as he had been visiting our home in the Yoke Powercam camp and seemed to have been after Therese to no avail. He must then have been fully aware of what had happened to Therese and of her whereabouts when he presented himself in the palace asking for her hand in marriage. How could Therese have said no to this long-sought door to her triumphant return to the coast? This marriage (like mine in Nwangong?) was clearly being entered into not for the sake of actually marrying but just as a stepping stone to something else. Was In-Law Nkengafac just foolish or did the groom think he could change things with time and marital stay? In-Law Nkengafac (like me) speedily did all what he needed to do and was on his way with his wife, really excited and pumped up; believing he had all reasons to be so. His conquered and won wife was not only from a reputable family, she was not only very pretty, she was just as tall as himself and here he was at long last married to the woman he must have been dying for, for such a long, long time. Was this not a dream come true?

But I am sure that, without Aunty Nzouata and the happy endings coming with her, In-Law Nkengafac would still be regretting his action even in his grave. Already in Meanja (Muyuka), Therese became his worst nightmare; hell broke loose, some would say. I would not want to get very deep into the man's agony but just imagine an excited man who brings his friends and other co-workers home, enthusiastically introducing his very beautiful wife to them only to be embarrassed with: "Who are you calling your wife, you fool? So you really thought I could marry you...?" After torturing the man for a while with hunger (she cooked alright but always ate everything and washed the pots before his arrival), fights, and all, Therese then left his house and went to Kumba where she became an *ashawo* or a sex worker.

Meanwhile In-Law Nkengafac, after many abortive visits to my father in Yoke (whose repeated response was 'I did not marry anyone to you'), made it to the palace to have the bride-prize returned. My grandpa is known for never asking for repayment of, or repaying, such a thing. Publicly scolding In-Law Nkengafac and regretting for having given his granddaughter to someone who was incapable of handling her, grandpa asked him to quickly go and assume his responsibilities. The mere thought of confronting Therese must have been just too much for this man who publicly broke into tears, pleading with the Fon that he could stand any other woman, not Therese. Then go and look for that other woman because, as far as the bride-prize goes, there is no discussion between us, the Fon said. I do not exactly know what happened next; whether the Fon/In-Law Nkengafac chose her for replacement or Aunty Nzouata herself opted to be. The important thing is that she became the new wife for the unreturned bride-prize.

I do not think I know many people in the Fossungu royal family that did not ridicule Aunty Nzouata's behaviour and marriage. But all through that she, like Foletia, stood firmly with her husband. Sticking it out together, the pair has been very successful in these marriage and family matters probably because it was Aunty Nzouata's choice (as Prince Nico Mbarga puts it in his musical piece, *Na My Choice*) to be the replacement and she was thus bold and truthful in that regard. She has consequently achieved a lot in the domain that many (including me with the 'longest-book' head) in the royal family are yet to attain: children and grandchildren who are well educated and professionals, and especially a home, out of the palace, for her own mother when grandpa died in 1979. Many of grandpa's wives that did not want to continue as his successor's wives had to choose grandpa's other children for husbands (like Uncle Ntimah's mother, Mami Cecilia, chose papa) in order to get out of the palace. But Aunty Nzouata's mum did not have to choose between the devil and the devil since she was able to move to her daughter's where she was accepted and more comfortable.

Even when my own birth mother (Mami Regina) and blood brother were chased out of my birth father's compound by an uncle, they had to be given a place in the palace (even though she was not 'officially' then Fon's wife) just because they had nowhere else to go to; and my birth mother continues to date perching at homes that are not mine or Dieudonné's. Yet, in order to preclude me from ever helping any other person outside her brothers, sisters, parents, and herself, Scholastica would run back to court in 2007 in Canada asking for *increase* in the child support amount because "He is building houses in Cameroon." This comportment, coming from a woman I have devoted the best part of my fifty-three years moulding and improving, can only lead me to suspect that it is someone else, not her, who decided that Scholastica accept to be my wife.

The Peter-Scholastica Marriage Decision

That marriage decision being first and foremost the parties' was not the case in the marital union between Scholastica and Peter could be seen in the parental spell and the court action already talked about in chapter 3. While the Foletia example noted above deals with tradition trying to hinder their decision already taken between themselves will be contrasted with others below (notably Uncle Ngufor's), I must precise here that in my case I never had that chance to even reach the decision with my wife-to-be *before* confronting the parents, a fact that might have worsened matters notwithstanding the marriage being one of a kind. I had been hearing a lot about Scholastica from her relations in Yaoundé after I returned from Alberta but I never really gave it serious thought. When I visited Nwangong in July 1993, a male cousin of mine again brought up the issue, even promising to accompany me to Fontem so that "you could see for yourself." Why not give it a try since I was already there in the village, I told myself.

It was on a Sunday that we arrived in Fontem, after hours of a bad or near inaccessible road. There was a football match in town and while at the pitch, I was discretely shown the girl in question. I

151

liked what I saw immediately and asked my companion to lead me to their place of abode after the match. Love at first sight. That evening we were welcomed to the Asahchop's and convinced not to drive back to Nwangong that night as we had intended doing. We were there alright but the problem was that I did not want to start talking possibility of marriage with the parents without having heard from Scholastica herself. I therefore tried to get her aside to discuss with just her but was insistently told that she and her father had no secrets so that whatever I had for her ears was good also for the father's. Well, it obviously was not working like I would have preferred but I still moved on to the point and said what I had to say to the hearing of both, including my companion. Was that not really the breaking of a golden rule (on my part) that was surely to lead directly to catastrophe? In other words, why did I waive the aforementioned two-party decision logic here? Could the Scholastica situation be distinguished on its merits?

I guess the decision for Scholastica to accept to marry me was that of the father who (unlike his daughter and I) seemed to have had detailed knowledge of who I was and where I was coming from. Could all the talk I had been hearing gratuitously about Scholastica in Yaoundé and the village have been planted? In short, could Scholastica's father have then simply seen the rare window to a brighter future for *his* family in me? That being the case (as it seems to be) is not any problem to me though; my mission in life being to ameliorate the lives of the greatest number of persons possible, my in-laws included. The point I am making here though is simply that parents (and you can be sure there are a lot of them) sometimes use the children, knowingly or otherwise, to further their own selfish agendas, not bothering about the child's own feelings, interests and future. This often occurs because most of the children themselves do not know themselves. Consequently, they are not bold and truthful; easily confounding the fear of their parents and other siblings with respect. This fact, by itself, spells a lot of disaster; and this holding true no matter what the bold and truthful partner does to have the marriage; or, if it is had through scheming, to keep it on track.

My 1993 traditional marriage to Scholastica became the talk of the day in the entire village as well as in Douala where I was then residing, and beyond. This was not just because of the seeming appropriateness of the duo – a factor that, itself alone, raised a lot of hope in regard of the many good things to come to the lives of many. The marriage was much-talked-about also because of several other factors that include (a) my previous declarations at an earlier spouse quest, and (b) the marriage style and close-knit relations, spiced by the honeymoon in Yaoundé and the Edmonton Connection.

The Declaration at Previous Spouse Quest

Most of the issues here relate to my general non-restrictive perspective on the matter and life generally; but particularly to some previous declarations made in Nwangong during Uncle Ngufor's quest for a spouse. As I said earlier, a quick contrasting example to Foletia is Uncle Ngufor who met and fell in love with a Balondo girl who almost had a baby with him but for miscarriage. He refrained from marrying this lady whom he himself often admiringly described as "exceptionally good all-round"; this simply because she was not Bangwa and would not be accepted by the traditionalists of the Fossungu royal family. Therefore, the decision to marry, in Uncle Ngufor's view, is not his and the girl's but that of the extended family; his comportment in the Justine palaver also confirming. You are about to know the amount of problems he encountered thereafter trying to marry and actually marrying a lady from Bangwa that led to my famous declaration.

It was late 1981 and we had been in the village for longer than expected because each visit to Maria's parents' home came up with new and unexpected demands for so and so relation that must first be satisfied; or this and that thing that has to be done first before the entire process (that I thought was nearing its end) can be begun! It was such agony, especially for someone like me who, to begin with, would be used to straight talk, and was not used to these kinds of back-and-forth near deceptive dealings. As we (the delegation from

153

Douala) were sitting one day in the palace with Fon DF Fossungu and other village dignitaries wondering aloud what could be the next move, I declared: "Frankly, ladies and gentlemen, if this is actually what it entails marrying a woman in Bangwa, then you all had better count me out." You can then see why my marrying not only a Bangwa in November 1993 but also doing so in the village and according to traditional rites has to be much talked about; especially again as my departure for Canada in September 1991 had pushed so many to the conclusion that I was surely going to marry an *oyibo* or white person, a point that lucidly brings in another uncle before further discussion of how this spouse episode moved Uncle Ngufor from a monogamist to polygamist.

Marrying a White Person

If the thought of marrying outside the ethnic group has terrified traditionalists, the thought of taking a white for spouse has often been devastating to the point of even causing people to miss great opportunities associated to travelling abroad or to the white man's country. This was particularly the case with Uncle Ntimah who I met in the household in Victoria on my arrival there. Extremely intelligent and sharp, he was just not lucky to continue to secondary school in the household. I never got the chance to know him there but did so while in Douala with them during my Roaming Days (after high school). I never heard Uncle Ntimah complaining about *EN* (papa's nickname from them) as I did in Yaoundé from his pal, Michael Njumo, who seems to have gotten the best staying in the household. Michael's description of *EN* would give you the impression that *EN* was all evil, without anything good about him. I used to listen to him in Yaoundé and just wondered if it is the fear of papa (the invisible hand behind his nickname) that caused him not to better evaluate my father. Was Uncle Ntimah not similarly describing the man who brought both of them up because he understood him better?

There was truly something magical about Uncle Ntimah's intelligence and speechmaking as well as his air of royalty. I was always struck by the way the rowdy Douala (Nwangong) meeting

154

house always went silent whenever he took the floor to talk. There is even rumour that Fon ST Fossungu had slated him for successor, especially as Mami Cecilia (his mom) was amongst my grandpa's favourite wives; and that it is the reason Uncle Ntimah was sent to be trained by papa who had, from the onset, shown no interest in the position. It is also generally said that papa too did not want the position principally because of his wife's (Mami Thecla's) opposition hinged on the thesis that, if papa were the Fon, his enormous wealth would be confused for that of Nwangong or the Fossungu family. Whatever it was, the King Solomon of Nwangong left the position to papa to do whatever he wanted with it, hoping perhaps that my father would in the end see the need to be the central pillar of the family. But, like the British heir who preferred his American woman to the crown, papa transferred the crown to one of his brothers, Fon DF Fossungu. This is a decision many (in and out of Nwangong) have trenchantly criticised; saying papa should instead have chosen a younger and more educated person in order to change the dynamics in Nwangong as was then happening in other Bangwa fondoms. That is the chitchat.

But it must also be remembered from the nickname Therese gave him that educated Uncle Anamoh was already referring to himself as 'chief' even as his father, Fon ST Fossungu, was still alive. Up to date, with two fons after his father, he is still causing trouble in Nwangong, claiming that he is the rightful person to be on the throne, and not the current Fon NN Fossungu. The people trenchantly criticising papa's decision may have some foundation for their disparagement; but just imagine what educated Uncle Anamoh, with his well known "treetop" mentality, would have done as the Fon of Nwangong and then you would have learned that, important as it may seem, formal education alone is just not enough for good and sapient leadership.

As brilliant as he was, Uncle Ntimah could not continue to secondary school like his colleague, my mother's brother, who then proceeded to BIROCOL (Bishop Rogan College in Buea). Uncle Ntimah later became a cook to a white family who liked both the

155

quality of his services and his character so much that in the 70s they wanted him to go along with them when they had to leave Cameroon and go back to Britain. Uncle Ntimah lost the chance of a lifetime (that would also have made him the very first in the family to travel to the Whiteman's land) simply because both his father and mother could not even entertain the idea; their principal, if not the only, concern being the 'abomination' of "Ntimah bringing us a white woman as his wife." This traditional perception is heavily based on the traditionalists' belief that white people not only have very unfamiliar ways but also do (1) break marriages (divorce) for what Africans generally see as frivolous reasons; (2) want everything for themselves, to the total exclusion of the other's (African's) extended family members; this being tied to (3) their very limited definition of family to be just husband, wife, and their children.

My marriage to Scholastica highly exhibits the first two reasons and has in a way also paradoxically "broken virgin grounds" by altering this worldview in the village of Nwangong particularly and Cameroon generally since many are now wont to cite our marriage saying: 'If a marriage like this is producing only what we are seeing, then let that child get his/her wife or husband from wherever; white, black, Chinese or whatever.' I will be coming back shortly to their use of *a marriage like this* (close-knit relations) after showing how my declaration in the village in regard of Uncle Ngufor's wife quest was just as prophetic as papa's *Book of Life and Death* questioning noted in Chapter 1, transforming a monogamist at heart to a polygamist of circumstances.

From Monogamy to Polygamy

As complicated as the marriage process is usually made in Bangwa (more on the issue can be found in Brain (1972)), events have subsequently shown that Uncle Ngufor's wife expedition had an additional scheming catch that further complicated the heartbreaking complication. This untruthful and devilish twist was in the nature of his own traditional father (in the sense of being successor to the biological father of both – Fon DF Fossungu) wanting the same girl

156

for himself at the same time as he was 'playing' the traditional role of prospective father-in-law. Stabbing in the back can hardly describe this enough. Uncle Ngufor and Maria loved each other so much and, because there seemed to be no headway in the matter even after many other trips Uncle Ngufor made to the village, he some time later eloped with Maria to Douala. Could Fon DF Fossungu then have felt the same way a man would, knowing his wife has run off with another 'inferior' man? The story even goes that Maria's father, who really wanted to be a father-in-law but to the Fon (how prestigious for him), openly performed cursing rites on his own daughter, leading to her not being able to bear a child for her husband of choice for as long as he (Maria's father) was alive. Wow! Why could both fathers here not have been as bold and truthful as to tell both children what they really wanted rather than allowing their children to be playing with two double-sided cutlasses?

Of course, Uncle Ngufor is a very patient person; but patience has its limits. Of course, again, very few are the African men who get married without the central issue being to have children. Without a child of his own for so long with Maria, Uncle Ngufor brought in his *njumba* who was carrying a baby for him. Although Maria (be careful here with the similar names) was not really the fighting type, Mary from the Northwest Region (the *njumba*-turned wife) never stopped insulting her with the fact that she was barren. Things only went from bad to worse in Uncle Ngufor's home, turning this fine gentleman into a heavy drinker and what have you. But as they say, providence has its unique way of correcting some of these things. By the time Mary was carrying her second child, Maria was also pregnant with her first. Could the (two-sided cutlasses') clock's hands have been turned back then? Is the truthfulness (or otherwise) of parents and other relations also one of the many things that have made the Peter-Scholastica marriage to be so especially atypical? What about the close-knit relations too?

Marriage Style and Close-Knit Relations

To avoid most of the complications and other deceptive practices associated with the marriage process in Bangwa, my father and I had told the other family to consolidate all that was demanded and present as a block. The reasoning, we had explained to them, was that this was an incomparable occasion for merrymaking and eliminating these matters that are so time-consuming gives more time for the guests and us all to have the fun that was deserving of the ceremony. The idea sold quickly because, as Fonenge had tersely observed, "it is all within the house and I don't particularly see any room and need for dragging matters. Do I not speak for both sides?" The others had concurred that he was right. I will here be critically looking at whether and how far the union was actually 'within the house' as presented, before looking at the style employed that led to the description of the union as 'ground-breaking', including the honeymoon to Yaoundé and the Edmonton connexion.

'Marrying Within the House' and 'Ground-Breaking Marriage'

Fonenge was correct in his claims because his household was clearly on both sides: he is my paternal uncle and his wife is Scholastica's maternal aunty, making their children cousins to both Scholastica and I. Ground-breaking as well? I was therefore marrying my cousin's cousin just as Scholastica was. But that is about as much as being on both sides goes because, for example, most of those children (the boys particularly) from this double-cousin household that orchestrated the chasing of the village nurse (who had become my friend and was taking especial care of my birthmother) out of Nwangong and her job were clearly not considering the "cousinness" from the Fossungu side. Also, during my Montréal traditional marriage, all the Fossungus and close relatives of the bride were supposed to occupy the 'high table' but Violet preferred staying in an obscure part of the hall, most probably because of Scholastica's attempts to dissuade people from attending and making the occasion

158

as grand as it was. Again, I have since been going to Cameroon but no Fonenge (child, mother, or father) has ever really taken any interest in knowing from me what happened to "their two-sided" ground-breaking relationship; most probably taking the Asahchop gossiping/blackmailing gospel as the only and correct version. That may not be surprising since it is from the Asahchop side that they profited when the suggested 'marriage block demand' was honoured without any change or argument by the Fossungu side; which brings me again to the parental spell (boldness and truthfulness).

Many of our acquaintances are yet to clearly understand why someone like me who love Scholastica as much should, in return, only get what I have this far gotten from her. From my understanding of people such as I learned from quickly comprehending my father, Scholastica is a very good person and wife. I know that well enough. She has simply fallen under the spell of her parents. Apparently, problems developed with Scholastica due to two principal facts that also highly challenge the concept of "marriage within the house": the four-year parental spell and the Kelie imbroglio. The second factor that is apparently given as aggravating things with Scholastica relates to my being upfront with her in revealing the truth about Kelie's paternity (as I had lately learnt). I had this knowledge while Scholastica was still in Cameroon but only discussed it with her when she had arrived in Canada through my tireless effort. Should I have then kept the fact that I was Kelie's biological father a secret, as had been requested by Kelie's mother (Odette Ateafac)? If others think so, I do not; and this is a particular problem I also have with Henriette Flavie Bayiha who is also mother of two of my children – Peter Ateh-Afac Fossungu, Jr., and Peteraf Karlemon-Ethan Tale'eh Fossungu. Flavie lied about everything from begin to end, including even lying about her two children in Cameroon. Lying especially about my child is something I made clear to Odette I would never do in any circumstances. Odette (Kelie's mom) is either Scholastica's aunty or cousin although Scholastica always presents her as her 'sister' – making sure to also

159

make it to look as if I was already married to her (Scholastica) and then had "a child with my sister."

Odette herself also surprises me a lot not only by her fear of the truth, a fact that is responsible for the child's information not just tying in; but also by her bizarre comportment. Odette is the most selfless and the most hardworking woman (my birth mother apart, perhaps) that I have ever encountered. In addition to her beauty, experience and maturity, what other woman than this would 'a man of many' like me want for a wife? But Odette refused my proposal for marriage because, in her own words, "I am too old for you." Where did she get the information that she was older than me, when I have come to know that we were both born in 1960? Was someone else 'within the house' putting these words into her mouth or was Odette simply taking the fact of her then having four children (three boys and a girl) as evidence of her being older than me? You will appreciate the importance of these questions if you realize that Odette and I fell for each other on first sight at a community event and instantly and very naturally came together and clicked in. And all this happened publicly despite the enormous pressures she had been under (since losing her husband) from older male members of the Douala Bangwa community. Was Odette also subsequently trying to hide her hidden age from me through her refusal to let me have Kelie's information? Was she under some sort of menace 'within the house'? I ask this particular question because, otherwise, who actually should normally be talking about her being too old for me as a spouse: I or her? Yet she went ahead and carried a baby for me, unknown to me. It was unknown to me because when my proposal was rejected on the age score, I began looking elsewhere. When I later saw Odette with a protruding stomach, I thought it was the handiwork of someone 'her age', not even suspecting in the least that I was actually that someone "her age". What could be behind all the needless lies?

Trying to answer this question is where this 'marrying within the house' thing takes another funny duress twist. When I sat Odette down in Douala in October 2002 (after my dad's burial) to

160

understand her side of the drama, she explained, first, that she was not sure that I was serious about the marriage talk. Bullshit, some would say. Just how serious should a man be in telling a woman (and especially one he is already dating) that he wants to marry her? How serious was I when I talked marriage to Scholastica-and-father that I had not even dated? Does Odette really know what she wants or who she is? Was she, for even a second, considering the interests and future of her four children from her first and dead husband? Anyway, listen to her response to the next enquiry. Why were you carrying a baby for me but did not tell me even when I was inviting you to my marriage with your niece? Her explanation: "I did not want to be seen as the one who spoiled my sister's marriage. In addition, I had realized then that I had made a big error in not taking your proposal to me seriously but was then happy that you were still marrying in my family. Was I supposed to have deprived the family of that?"[16]Does it not smell like some threats 'within the house' were hanging over this lady? Frankly, had I been someone with a temper, I would, at that point, have been throwing some blows at Odette. But would that have changed anything, including the ground-breaking marriage to her niece?

Everything was so speedily and efficiently done during the traditional marriage with Scholastica. When the Master of Ceremony and Chief Celebrant in the person of Foletia announced the commencement of the traditional rites, some people who had been seeing themselves as going to profit through being the usual go-betweens demanded how that could be when they had not yet performed their task. Foletia had not been chosen for the post by his friend, the bride's father, for nothing. He is well known to handle such matters with a lot of style that blends tradition and modernity in a way unique to Foletia. I also remember him well at the burial of

---

[16]I could only then begin to see why Odette did not even attend the wedding in the village and why I was only told by her that Kelie is my child while I was in Canada (despite that she was born while I still was in Douala) and with the request to keep it a secret (to who?); punctuated with all the falsification of the child's birth information, twisted information that I only got in 2010.

papa in October 2002 giving his dead brother's biography. Having outlined the children papa left behind, for example, he had added:

Those were his birth children but as you may want to know he did not consider as children only those that carried his genes; and if I want to outline all of those, it would be two or three days from today and I would still be doing just that. If you may permit me to cite just a few of them, then take a good look at Peter Ateh-Afac from Canada at whom the camera is now pointing. Don't mind his height because, as short as you may find him, the book that is in his head is longer than you can ever measure. Who do you think brought him up? It is Forbehndia. Also consider Marie-Claire who is in the United States of America, one of the many children in this royal family who do not even know their real fathers and mothers, it is Forbehndia who brought her up ....

I do not truly know any event that has taken place in Nwangong in particular without Foletia's front-row participation and my marriage there could not have been that exception. Answering the questions of the side-stepped and perplexed go-betweens, Foletia had (prophetically) stated:

You people have been invited here today to a ground-breaking marriage ceremony. If you pay the required attention and stop unnecessarily hunting for just something to eat or drink (there is more than enough of that too), you will not only learn a lot but also keep track of what is happening here. What your question is about has already been put behind us. Isn't it said by our elders that when your relative is up on the plume tree you normally eat the blackest plumes? Our son here has been to other lands and are we not witnessing a new and more progressive way of doing things? This is indeed what some of you are wont to describe as 'a Whiteman marriage'. Therefore, people of Nwangong, do pay attention while we move on with the modernized traditional rites of marriage. I must have to divulge a secret here though, namely, that the two families that have invited us here have insisted to me that they do not want any of you to

162

eat cold food at this ceremony, or be able to walk home tomorrow after the dancing that is awaiting your feet in particular.

There had been sporadic applause as he had been speaking and the 'divulged secret' carried it to a thunderous pitch. But where would my own boldness and truthfulness be hiding? All through Foletia's speech my head had been turning something over: Why was I marrying my cousin's cousin on the same spot I had desperately fallen in love with my cousin (not knowing then she was my cousin) who had thrown me into a marriage trance some years earlier? But when Foletia talked of divulging a secret I was startled and wondered what would happen if I stopped him at that very moment and divulged the following secret to him, to the hearing of the entire gathering:

But for a tradition that allows an uncle of mine to take my mother as wife but precludes me from marrying an uncle's daughter, you, Foletia, would next be handing the glass of palm wine but to your own daughter to drink and then pass the rest over to you as her father to also drink to indicate that she has accepted from the bottom of her heart to be my wife; and the second glass but to your wife to drink and pass the rest to you as her husband indicating that both of you have given your blessings to your daughter's choice to be my wife; and, on my side, to the same people here now present to indicate that I have, from the most sacred part of my heart, chosen her for my wife and they have bountifully accorded their blessings to that choice.

What marriage on earth would have been more ground-breaking and with more close-knit relations than this? Where were the boldness and truthfulness this time in me? In other words, why on earth did I let go the person that brought about the marriage turn-around rather than 'break virgin ground' by altering that tradition that does not also prohibit my marrying my cousin's cousin? Of course, I

163

would very easily have sent that tradition packing, especially as Foletia (being heavily pivotal here) is not only one of the most progressive in the royal family but also himself a tradition breaker. On his and wife's side, I did not see any real problem; the real issue having to do with the girl's age and the handicap of not knowing how I feel for her. I like to be reasonably bold, to leave out 'respectful boldness'; the cases in point being the reasoning with the dean of the UNIYAO Faculty of Laws and Economics, and with papa regarding the tenants. In view of the girl's age at the time I miraculously and dreadfully fell in love with her, there is just no way that I could possibly have been reasoning with anyone, not even progressives like Foletia. That is precisely why I did not talk about it anymore with my birth mother even after having promised showing her the girl in question. Could Mami Regina have been intelligently aware of the situation?

Second, to be able to successfully fight the tradition-breaking war, the girl and I needed to have made the marriage decision together. (Why did I have to ignore the initial decision requirement in Scholastica's case?) Put differently, I needed to be on the same side with the girl fighting as a team; otherwise, it would be like fighting a lost battle. How else could I have gotten the girl on my side of the fight in the first place when she did not even know how I felt about her? Or could she have known, viewing the manner she had thrown me off balance and into that marriage trance even at her very tender age? Why would I want to think that she couldn't have known without also getting that from the horse's own mouth?

All this reasonable-boldness stuff would apply though only at the time I first saw my young cousin; not at all to the time of my marrying Scholastica since my cousin was then seventeen and just three years younger than Scholastica. The most important question becomes that of why on my return from Edmonton I had chickened out from challenging tradition and instead going after women that clearly were not meant for me? Why did I not then squarely confront my lioness (like me, my cousin is also an August-born) with my deeply-embedded feelings for her? Why was I not bold and truthful

164

then and could my marriage messes so far be her unique magical way of bringing me "home to me" (to borrow from my Manjo girlfriend)? Paradoxical, isn't it?

The Paradoxes of 'A Whiteman Marriage'

I was hardly conversant with the traditional marriage ceremony proper in Nwangong and had expected to be shown this or that. But all that was unnecessary, thanks to Foletia's efficient and innovative blending of both official (that I knew well) and traditional practices to produce what was simply a unique and easy-to-follow process. But that alone does not seem to give the Scholastica-Peter marriage the epithet of "a Whiteman marriage". Africans (or limit it to Cameroonians that I know well) are known to describe something well done with the Whiteman; for example, "He drives like a Whiteman", "I did it like a White". Is it not purely paradoxical that these people would like the way the Whites go about marrying but would not tolerate their relations marrying a White? That they would also like living in the 'Whiteman's country' that is heavily founded on the 'Time is Money' principles but always content themselves with their BMT (Black Man Time)? I find it amazing that most (Black) Africans have decided to immigrate and live in "the Whiteman's country" but always content themselves with this brainless BMT cover for their gross irresponsibility. Imagine being invited to a ceremony billed for 8 PM. You arrive at 7.55 PM and the hosts themselves are not even ready; and then the occasion ends up beginning at 11 PM, and when you are wondering if your wrist watch had three hours advance and all you get is that 8 PM in BMT is about midnight. What rubbish!

Was there not a lot of prophesy in the 'Whiteman marriage' description as well – a forecast hinging on the paradoxes of the Scholastica-Peter union? That seems to be the case, leading to the change in the worldview in the village on marrying outside it. The three factors cited earlier as being responsible for Africans despising marriage to a white person can show how and why; with the

165

exception of some aggravating circumstances in Scholastica's definition of family that does not fit into the Whiteman's at all, nor the African's. Also worth noting is the fact that a White lady always makes sure to put the targeted father in a comfortable position to pay it before going ahead to demand for child custody and child support from him. Scholastica and her parents did not do so by her refusing to sponsor me to become a Canadian permanent resident; which clearly points to the fact that she and her directing parents see child support as a means of enrichment and/or punishment or destruction rather than a responsibility. In addition, what was/is actually the basis of Scholastica's divorce claim, quite apart from the desire to extract so-called child support?

Scholastica's eyes and ears are all over the place (in both Cameroon and Canada) nosing for information about any possibility of my aiding anyone else, including my own children and birth mother. It is clear that Scholastica's "eyes and ears all over" (including the 'double-sided cousins') did not target only the beneficiaries of the unmet promise (made during the Generator Ceremony in Nwangong) – the youths of Nwangong especially – but also Queenta (the intelligent nurse)and by extension, my birth mother who she then began taking care of. Seemingly under instruction, Scholastica's eyes and ears in Cameroon orchestrated Queenta's being chased out of Nwangong and of her job in the same way they have been doing to any woman in Canada that tries to associate with me. All this would happen because only her parents, brothers, and sisters are important as her family; a point reinforced by her back-stabbing dealings with the wife of Solo who organized the Yaoundé Honeymoon. Do some of these people ever for one minute think of the saying: 'Do unto others what you would want done unto you'? This question is particularly significant if you realize that one of Scholastica's conspicuous three email signatures is: "Be a blessing and a positive force wherever you go." Indeed.

166

Conclusion

The most appropriate conclusion to this book that I would have given, given the opportunity to break virgin ground by breaking long-established tradition, would be to ask you to begin reading again from the first page to this one; or to just repeat here that "If you are destined for greatness, the only obstacle that can prevent you from becoming great is you" and that is it. Not having been accorded that opportunity to break tradition here (since I have embraced it by beginning with a traditional Introduction), I must highlight a few points by way of conclusion, knowing still that you are very entitled to draw your own conclusions for yourself.

This book has given you some of the 'Becoming Better' battles that I have fought in view of making things better for the greatest number of persons possible: despite the money and other handicaps resulting from some exclusionist definitions of family. Money, as essential as it is, does not become too essential an ingredient of success to those who really want to achieve their objectives; as they would still achieve – with or without it. When I look back therefore and see how much I have had to be helped in various ways by several people, some of them being complete strangers to me, I cannot help but be optimistic and fortified that I shall one day carry my objective of "making life more worthwhile for the greatest number of persons possible" to a much higher level or platform; and this notwithstanding the obstacles so far encountered (because of the way family and/or children has been defined by those I dearly love) and those that are still, or will be, standing in the way. Always be grateful and thankful from the bottom of your heart therefore for every act of help that comes your way. It is because of this mannerism that I was able, for instance, to make the discovery regarding the BIROCOL money affair; and also able to extricate myself from the Takum (Nigeria) dire straits.

I think most of papa's relations that came to live in the household could not stay (difficult as the household was) principally because they did not know themselves nor have clear objectives with which they identified; leading them to be unable to look at the larger picture; and thus becoming bitter over little things – a trait that prevented most of them from becoming better. Bitterness that is not born out of the truth will only consume you before the real obstacle itself shows up for that purpose. In my drive to becoming better, I learnt a lot from the experiences of two of my uncles in the household to whom papa offered two different positions of yard boy and of driver, respectively (and their various opposing responses to him, as well as the ensuing consequences on their evolution. Once you know yourself and have objectives with which you identify, you will often quickly and almost instinctively find a way to get out of situations that hinder the attainment of your goals. You consequently look at the big picture, not the small. That is why the funny definition of family in Canada did not just push me to be reactionary but to continue with what I thought was the best option for the future of the children, including those people that the strange definition was geared toward 'advancing'. The same reasoning applied to many other situations in Cameroon as well as in Montreal.

My knowledge of some of the things that have enormously aided and will continue helping me succeed in life has been brought about by many people, both within and outside my large and extended royal family. I have all through the longest short-cut to university education and marriage/family highlighted the contribution of the many early influences that have helped in my progress. In the family, I cannot escape specific mention of my two mothers and one of my two fathers, as well as uncles (like Foletia, Ngufor, and Fonge) and aunts (such as Tumekong and Nzouata) and other siblings of the household. I particularly learn to lot from Therese's tragedy just as I am expecting a lot of people would learn a lot from my story's successes and failures.

When you know who you are and what you are up to and up against, you will often correctly anticipate a problem before it actually comes and the whole story illustrates that there is nothing as easy as solving a problem that pops up when you are ready for it. What

168

makes a problem really scary is when it takes you by surprise and you are caught off guard. And, truly, Scholastica's definition of family in Canada really caught me off guard and its implications would have been even more catastrophic but for the fact that I am a 'man of many' and, therefore, look at the larger picture of things. To a larger picture person, for example, money is not all that is necessary for success; honouring one's engagement with others is also very important since it is in a way making life much more meaningful to the many people behind you by not burning the bridge after you have crossed it.

In another sense, you also should not let something that happened to you in the past completely determine the present and future because there are many doors to happiness; meaning that when one door is closed many more are still open. An open-minded person hardly respects a tradition that is not progressive; a trait that largely explains why it is open-minded people who are mostly associated with the breaking of virgin grounds (pioneers); when you look at the larger picture, you visualize things more clearly than those who look at the narrow. Learning early to depend on you and not being bitter when disappointed as I did has proven to be one of my greatest ingredients in overcoming adversity in life; because bitterness consumes you even before the hardship being confronted can do so. Only those who cannot handle the truth get bitter because if you can handle bitterness, there will be no need for you yourself to become bitter. These are some of the things that go into the postulation that, if you are destined for great accomplishments, the only obstacle that can prevent you from becoming great is you. It is obvious that I would not have been able to build on what the experiences of the others in the household and other early influences (both in the village and in *ncheng*) provided if I did not know who I was and what I was up to; if I did not have an open mind or look at the larger picture of things; and if I did not have clear objectives with which I define myself, thus not knowing my worth and, consequently, was too afraid to break virgin grounds with professions.

169

Repetition has its positive aspects; and I would not mind reiterating here that if this book teaches parents generally but divorcing or divorced ones specifically that the future and interest of the children, whatever the cause of their going apart (or calculations for the non-divorcing others), should always be the prime mover for whatever arrangement (or decision) they do or should make, then it would have achieved one of its purposes. I think the world would be a better place if people generally look at the larger picture of things; because larger picture people are usually those that are better suited to give children, without definitional distinctions, a better or brighter future than what they themselves have, irrespective of the societies they live in. Should Social Work in Canada, as in Africa, and the rest of the world, not try to see to it that people working in this domain that has enormous powers to make or mar the future of children in particular be at least people who can truthfully attest to and pass the 'Charity begins at home' litmus test?

References

Anyangwe, Carlson. *The Magistracy and the Bar in Cameroon* (Yaounde: PANAG-CEPER, 1989).

Brain, Robert. *Bangwa Kingship and Marriage* (Cambridge: Cambridge University Press, 1972).

For-Mukwai, Gideon F. *Fighting Adversity with Audacity* (Bamenda, Cameroon: Langaa RPCIG, 2010).

Fossungu, Peter Ateh-Afac. *Understanding Confusion in Africa: The Politics of Multiculturalism and Nation-Building in Cameroon* (Bamenda, Cameroon: Langaa RPCIG, 2013a).

Fossungu, Peter Ateh-Afac. *Democracy and Human Rights in Africa: The Politics of Collective Participation and Governance in Cameroon* (Bamenda, Cameroon: Langaa RPCIG, 2013b).

Fossungu, Peter Ateh-Afac. "The ICAO Assembly: The Most Unsupreme of Supreme Organs in the United Nations System? A Critical Analysis of Assembly Sessions" 26 *Transportation Law Journal* (1998a), 1–49.

Fossungu, Peter Ateh-Afac. "Some Order in Cameroonian Names" *The Herald* N° 685 (11-12 November 1998b), 4.

www.ingramcontent.com/pod-product-compliance
Lightning Source LLC
Chambersburg PA
CBHW022318280326
41932CB00010B/1147